JERUSALEM

Illustrated History Atlas

Martin Gilbert

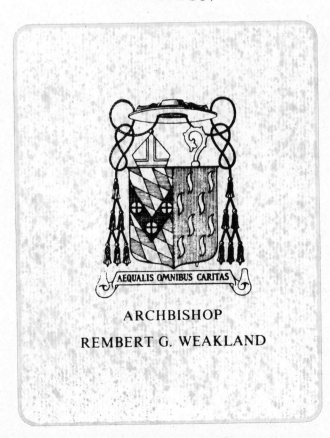

AEQUALIS OMNIBUS CARITAS

ARCHBISHOP
REMBERT G. WEAKLAND

Other Atlases by Martin Gilbert

Recent History Atlas 1860-1960
British History Atlas
American History Atlas
Jewish History Atlas
First World War Atlas
Russian History Atlas
The Arab-Israeli Conflict: Its History in Maps
The Jews of Arab Lands: Their History in Maps
The Jews of Russia: Their History in Maps and Photographs

Other Books by Martin Gilbert

Winston S. Churchill Volume III 1914-1916
            Companion Volume III (in two parts)
Winston S. Churchill Volume IV 1916-1922
            Companion Volume IV (in three parts)
Winston S. Churchill Volume V 1922-1939

The European Powers 1900-1945
The Roots of Appeasement
Sir Horace Rumbold: Portrait of a Diplomat
Churchill: A Photographic Portrait
Britain and Germany Between the Wars
Plough My Own Furrow: the Life of Lord Allen of Hurtwood
Servant of India: Diaries of the Viceroy's Private Secretary
Churchill (Spectrum Books)
Lloyd George (Spectrum Books)
Winston Churchill (Clarendon Biography)
Winston Churchill (Jackdaw)
The Coming of War in 1939 (Jackdaw)
The Second World War (for young readers)
The Appeasers (with Richard Gott)

British edition published by Martin Gilbert in conjunction with The Board of Deputies of British Jews, Woburn House, Upper Woburn Place, London W.C.1.

American and Canadian edition published by Macmillan Publishing Inc., 866 Third Avenue, New York NY 10022.

Israeli edition published by Steimatzky's Agency Limited, Jerusalem, Tel Aviv, and Haifa.

Preface

In this Atlas, I trace the history of Jerusalem from biblical times to the present day. For some years I have felt drawn to use the method of my previous historical atlases to try to portray something of the City's many trials and tribulations, and of the lives and experiences of its citizens through more than thirty centuries.

Each map is illustrated by a facing page of prints or photographs: the sixty-six maps, taken together, are intended to provide a broad survey of Jerusalem's history, with special emphasis on the City's development during the last hundred and fifty years, when it grew from a remote and impoverished provincial town of the Ottoman Empire, with a population of less than 40,000, to a capital City with a population of more than 360,000.

In the bibliography, beginning on page 124, I have listed those maps, atlases, guide books, travellers' tales and historical works which I consulted while preparing the maps, and on which I drew for the contemporary material which they contained for each decade of the City's history.

I am extremely grateful to all those individuals who gave me advice, encouragement and materials, both in London and Jerusalem, during my work on the maps and illustrations for this volume: in particular I should like to thank Azaria Alon, Professor Yehoshua Ben-Arieh, Ruth Chesin, Chaim Choref, Fritz Cohen, David S. Curtis, David Eldan, Oded Eran, Rabbi Hugo Gryn, Peter Halben, Mrs Adina Haran, Ya'acov Harlap, Dr Michael Heymann, Dr Benjamin Jaffe, Mrs Sheila Koretz, Henry Kendall, Teddy Kollek, Tomi Lamm, Menachem Levine, Irène Lewitt, G. Eric Matson, Margaret McAfee, Martin Paisner, Professor Leo Picard, Zev Radovan, David Rubinger, Michael Sacher, Hanna Safieh, Lord Samuel, Mrs Yael Vered, Dr Zev Vilnay, Mrs M. Wahl, Mrs Gillian Webster, Dr Martin Weil, Frank Wheeler, Professor Yigael Yadin, Sima Zelig, and Josef Zweig for their much appreciated help and guidance.

I should also like to thank those Libraries, Agencies and Institutions which have provided me with historical material, or with access to facts and documents, used or quoted in this atlas: The Anglo-Israel Association, London; the Bodleian Library, Oxford; the Central Zionist Archives, Jerusalem; the Elia Photo-Service, Jerusalem; the Embassy of the Hashemite Kingdom of Jordan, London; the Embassy of Israel, London; the Embassy of the United States of America, London; the Foreign and Commonwealth Office, London; the Government Press Office, Tel Aviv; the Imperial War Museum, London; Israel Information, London; the Israel Museum, Jerusalem; the Jerusalem Foundation; the *Jerusalem Post;* the Jewish Agency, Jerusalem; Keren Hayesod, Jerusalem; Keren Kayemet, Jerusalem; the Matson Photo Service, California; the Municipality of Jerusalem; the Palestine Exploration Fund, London; Ross Photo, Jerusalem; St. Antony's College, Middle East Centre, Oxford; *The Times;* and the United Nations, London.

I am also grateful to Miss Sue Townshend, for her secretarial help; to Jerry Moeran and Jean Hunt of Studio Edmark, Oxford, for copying many of the prints and photographs; to T.A. Bicknell, for his superb cartographic work over many months; and to my wife for her constant encouragement. As with each of my previous historical atlases, I should welcome from readers any corrections, suggested amendments, or ideas and materials for extra maps.

Martin Gilbert
Merton College, Oxford

28 March 1977

List of maps

List of maps

Plate 2   The rebuilding of Jerusalem under Nehemiah; a print published in 1705. "Come, and let us build up the wall of Jerusalem": Nehemiah, 2,17. "And the rulers of the people dwelt at Jerusalem: the rest of the people also cast lots, to bring one of ten to dwell in Jerusalem the holy city"., Nehemiah, 11,1.

JERUSALEM FROM ANCIENT TIMES TO THE DESTRUCTION OF THE SECOND TEMPLE IN 70 AD

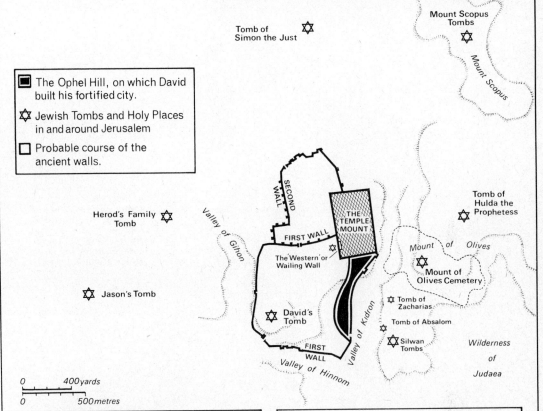

Jerusalem was an inhabited city in the early bronze age, well before 2500 BC. Later it was a Jebusite fortress. Conquered by the Jews under David, it became, from 1000 BC, the political and religious capital of the Jews. Here Solomon built the first Temple, and here the Jews were sovereign for more than 600 years, until the Babylonian conquest in 587 BC, when many Jews were slaughtered, and others sent to exile. Returning under the patronage of Persia fifty years later, the Jews, under Nehemiah, rebuilt their Temple, and restored the authority of Jerusalem as their religious centre.

Sanhedria Tombs

Mount Scopus Tombs

Tomb of Simon the Just

Mount Scopus

■ The Ophel Hill, on which David built his fortified city.

✡ Jewish Tombs and Holy Places in and around Jerusalem

☐ Probable course of the ancient walls.

SECOND WALL

THE TEMPLE MOUNT

Tomb of Hulda the Prophetess

Herod's Family Tomb

Valley of Gihon

FIRST WALL

The Western or Wailing Wall

Mount of Olives

Mount of Olives Cemetery

Jason's Tomb

David's Tomb

Tomb of Zacharias

Tomb of Absalom

Valley of Kidron

Silwan Tombs

Wilderness of Judaea

FIRST WALL

Valley of Hinnom

0   400 yards
0   500 metres

332 BC Alexander of Macedon conquers the City, and confirms the Jewish privileges granted by the Persians.

301 BC The Ptolemys of Egypt grant the Jews autonomy in domestic matters. Jewish social and religious life flourishes.

198 BC The Seleucid conquerors grant the Jews the right to live by 'the laws of their fathers'.

167 BC Antiochus IV suppresses Jewish religious practices, desecrates the Temple, confiscates its treasures, and converts it into a Greek shrine.

141 BC Jerusalem captured by the Jewish Hasmoneans, remaining their capital for 78 years. Jewish religious and commercial life flourished.

63 BC The Roman conquest. 12,000 Jews massacred in Jerusalem. The priests, who refused to halt the service, were killed while still praying at the Altar.

66 AD The revolt of the Jewish 'Zealots', who held Jerusalem for 4 years.

70 AD Romans reoccupy Jerusalem. The Temple destroyed and the city laid waste. Many Jews taken as captives to Rome.

Map 1   7

Plate 3   Two Jews from Bukhara, photographed in
Jerusalem in May 1950.
Driven from the land
of Israel more than 2,000
years before, the Jews of
Bukhara maintained their
religious traditions and
cultural identity: in 1892
a group of Bukharan
Jews returned to Jerusa-
lem (see Map 30), found-
ing a vigorous and flour-
ishing community there.

Plate 4   Titus, surprised by Jewish soldiers while viewing the city in 70AD; an engraving published in
1844. The Jewish historian Josephus wrote: "So this success of the Jews' first attack raised
their minds, and gave them ill-grounded hope; and this short inclination of fortune, on their
side, made them very courageous for the future."

8

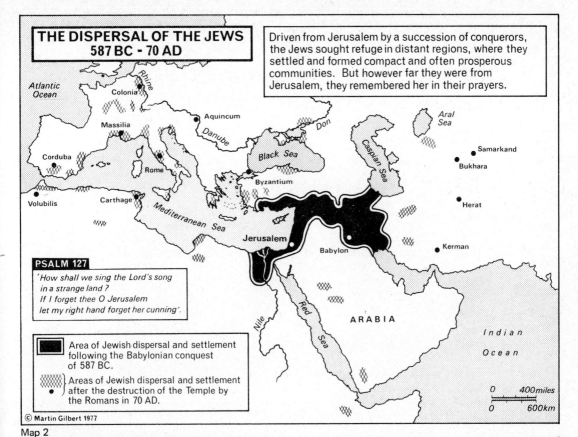

THE DISPERSAL OF THE JEWS 587 BC - 70 AD

Driven from Jerusalem by a succession of conquerors, the Jews sought refuge in distant regions, where they settled and formed compact and often prosperous communities. But however far they were from Jerusalem, they remembered her in their prayers.

PSALM 127

'How shall we sing the Lord's song in a strange land? If I forget thee O Jerusalem let my right hand forget her cunning'.

█ Area of Jewish dispersal and settlement following the Babylonian conquest of 587 BC.

▨ } Areas of Jewish dispersal and settlement after the destruction of the Temple by the Romans in 70 AD.

© Martin Gilbert 1977

0   400 miles
0   600 km

Map 2

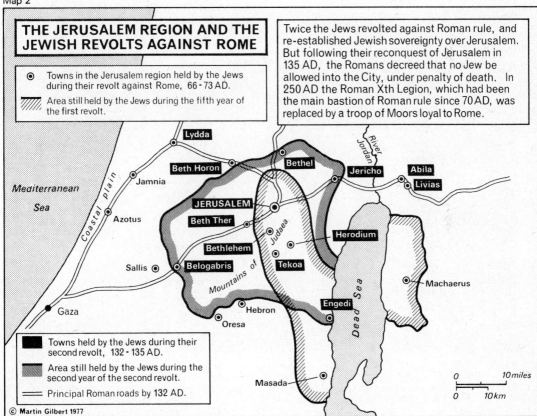

THE JERUSALEM REGION AND THE JEWISH REVOLTS AGAINST ROME

Twice the Jews revolted against Roman rule, and re-established Jewish sovereignty over Jerusalem. But following their reconquest of Jerusalem in 135 AD, the Romans decreed that no Jew be allowed into the City, under penalty of death. In 250 AD the Roman Xth Legion, which had been the main bastion of Roman rule since 70 AD, was replaced by a troop of Moors loyal to Rome.

⊙ Towns in the Jerusalem region held by the Jews during their revolt against Rome, 66 - 73 AD.

╱ Area still held by the Jews during the fifth year of the first revolt.

█ Towns held by the Jews during their second revolt, 132 - 135 AD.

▨ Area still held by the Jews during the second year of the second revolt.

── Principal Roman roads by 132 AD.

© Martin Gilbert 1977

0   10 miles
0   10 km

Map 3

9

Plate 5   The Altar of the Coptic Chapel in the Church of the Holy Sepulchre; a photograph taken in August 1967. The Chapel is one of several covering a large stone slab, said to be the very stone on which the body of Jesus was laid after it had been taken down from the Cross.

Plate 6   Russian pilgrims at the Monastery of the Cross; a photograph taken in about 1900. The Monastery was believed to be at the site of the tree used to make the cross on which Jesus was crucified. First built by Georgian monks in 300AD, it was sacked by the Arabs in 1099, but restored in 1644 by the King of Georgia.

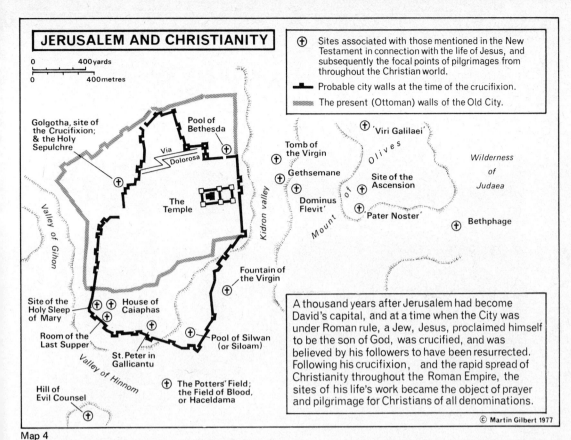

JERUSALEM AND CHRISTIANITY

0 ___ 400 yards
0 ___ 400 metres

✝ Sites associated with those mentioned in the New Testament in connection with the life of Jesus, and subsequently the focal points of pilgrimages from throughout the Christian world.

◼◼◼ Probable city walls at the time of the crucifixion.

░░░ The present (Ottoman) walls of the Old City.

Golgotha, site of the Crucifixion; & the Holy Sepulchre

Pool of Bethesda

Via Dolorosa

The Temple

Tomb of the Virgin

'Viri Galilaei'

Gethsemane

Site of the Ascension

Dominus Flevit'

Pater Noster'

Mount of Olives

Wilderness of Judaea

Bethphage

Kidron valley

Valley of Gihon

Fountain of the Virgin

Site of the Holy Sleep of Mary

House of Caiaphas

Room of the Last Supper

St. Peter in Gallicantu

Pool of Silwan (or Siloam)

Valley of Hinnom

Hill of Evil Counsel

✝ The Potters' Field; the Field of Blood, or Haceldama

A thousand years after Jerusalem had become David's capital, and at a time when the City was under Roman rule, a Jew, Jesus, proclaimed himself to be the son of God, was crucified, and was believed by his followers to have been resurrected. Following his crucifixion, and the rapid spread of Christianity throughout the Roman Empire, the sites of his life's work became the object of prayer and pilgrimage for Christians of all denominations.

© Martin Gilbert 1977

Map 4

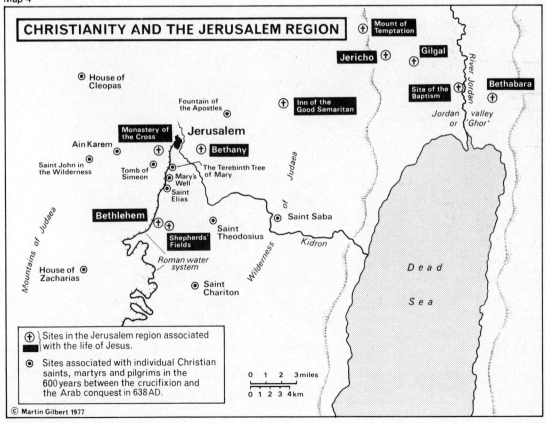

CHRISTIANITY AND THE JERUSALEM REGION

Mount of Temptation

Jericho

Gilgal

River Jordan

Bethabara

House of Cleopas

Fountain of the Apostles

Inn of the Good Samaritan

Site of the Baptism

Jordan valley or 'Ghor'

Monastery of the Cross

Jerusalem

Bethany

Ain Karem

Saint John in the Wilderness

Tomb of Simeon

Mary's Well

The Terebinth Tree of Mary

Judaea

Saint Elias

Bethlehem

Saint Saba

Mountains of Judaea

Shepherds' Fields

Saint Theodosius

Kidron

Dead

Roman water system

House of Zacharias

Saint Chariton

Wilderness

Sea

✝ Sites in the Jerusalem region associated with the life of Jesus.

◉ Sites associated with individual Christian saints, martyrs and pilgrims in the 600 years between the crucifixion and the Arab conquest in 638 AD.

© Martin Gilbert 1977

0 1 2 3 miles
0 1 2 3 4 km

Map 5

Plate 7   The Church of the Holy Sepulchre, from an engraving published in London in 1835.

Plate 8   Byzantine columns of the Church of the Virgin, photographed in 1893. With the Islamic Conquest of 629AD, the Church was converted into the Al Aksa mosque. These original columns were damaged in the earthquakes of 1927 and 1936, and replaced (see Map 38).

BYZANTINE JERUSALEM 324 AD - 629 AD

In 324 AD Jerusalem came under the rule, from Byzantium (later Constantinople), of the Christian Emperor Constantine. Two years later his mother Helena visited Jerusalem, where she 'located' several Christian sites and relics. The Temple of Venus was destroyed, the Church of the Holy Sepulchre dedicated on the same site in 335, and the Eleona Church built on the Mount of Olives.

———— The walls of Jerusalem in Byzantine times.

〰〰 The old Roman Aqueduct, kept under repair and continuing to bring water from Solomon's Pools in Byzantine times.

▨ Principal buildings constructed during Byzantine rule.

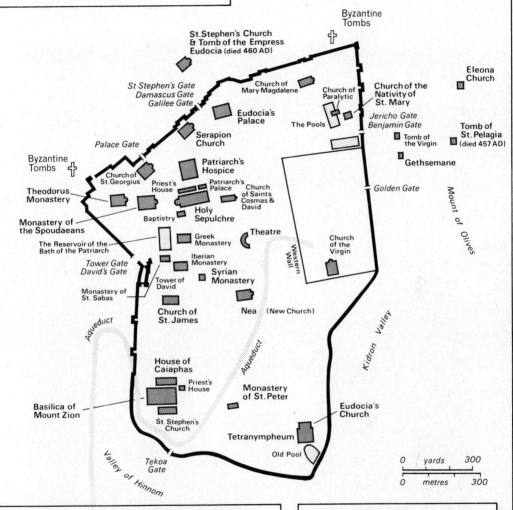

Byzantine Tombs

St.Stephen's Church & Tomb of the Empress Eudocia (died 460 AD)

Eleona Church

St Stephen's Gate
Damascus Gate
Galilee Gate

Church of Mary Magdalene

Church of Paralytic

Church of the Nativity of St. Mary

Eudocia's Palace

The Pools

Jericho Gate
Benjamin Gate

Tomb of St. Pelagia (died 457 AD)

Palace Gate

Serapion Church

Tomb of the Virgin

Gethsemane

Byzantine Tombs

Patriarch's Hospice

Church of St.Georgius

Priest's House

Patriarch's Palace

Church of Saints Cosmas & David

Golden Gate

Mount of Olives

Theodorus Monastery

Monastery of the Spoudaeans

Baptistry

Holy Sepulchre

The Reservoir of the Bath of the Patriarch

Greek Monastery

Theatre

Western Wall

Church of the Virgin

Tower Gate
David's Gate

Iberian Monastery

Syrian Monastery

Monastery of St. Sabas

Tower of David

Church of St. James

Nea (New Church)

Kidron Valley

Aqueduct

House of Caiaphas

Priest's House

Monastery of St. Peter

Eudocia's Church

Aqueduct

Basilica of Mount Zion

St. Stephen's Church

Tetranympheum

Old Pool

Valley of Hinnom

Tekoa Gate

| 0 | yards | 300 |
| 0 | metres | 300 |

Under Byzantine rule, several Roman families settled in the City, many Christian churches were founded, and the city was rebuilt within its walls. Jews were forbidden to enter the city except on the 9th of Av, when they were allowed to lament the destruction of the Temple. The Empress Eudocia, who first visited the city in 438, allowed the Jews to return. In 614 the Persians, having conquered the city, handed it over to the Jews. But with the return of the Byzantines in 629, the Jews were again expelled.

'On the 15th September, annually, an immense number of people of different nations are used to meet in Jerusalem for the purpose of commerce, and the streets are so clogged with the dung of camels, horses, mules and oxen, that they become almost impassable'.

BISHOP ARCULF OF GAUL 680 AD

© Martin Gilbert 1977

Map 6

13

Plate 9   The Dome of the Rock, and Haram (the Temple Mount of the Jews); from a photograph taken in 1871. The Dome, which was begun in 685AD and completed in 691, collapsed in 1016, but was reconstructed. The present 'golden' dome, of anodised aluminium, dates from 1956.

Plate 10   The Tomb of the Virgin, part of a Crusader church in the Kidron Valley, below the Mount of Olives, from a print from W.H. Bartlett, *Walks about the City and Environs of Jerusalem*, published in 1843. The original Church was built in 534AD during the Byzantine period, but was converted into a mosque in 637, following the Islamic conquest.

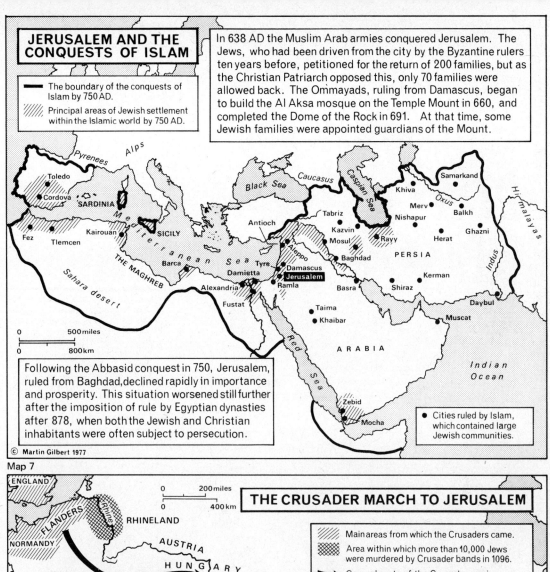

JERUSALEM AND THE CONQUESTS OF ISLAM

— The boundary of the conquests of Islam by 750 AD.

/// Principal areas of Jewish settlement within the Islamic world by 750 AD.

In 638 AD the Muslim Arab armies conquered Jerusalem. The Jews, who had been driven from the city by the Byzantine rulers ten years before, petitioned for the return of 200 families, but as the Christian Patriarch opposed this, only 70 families were allowed back. The Ommayads, ruling from Damascus, began to build the Al Aksa mosque on the Temple Mount in 660, and completed the Dome of the Rock in 691. At that time, some Jewish families were appointed guardians of the Mount.

Pyrenees · Alps · Toledo · Cordova · SARDINIA · Fez · Kairouan · SICILY · Tlemcen · THE MAGHREB · Barca · Mediterranean Sea · Sahara desert · Alexandria · Fustat · Damietta · Tyre · Ramla · Jerusalem · Damascus · Aleppo · Antioch · Black Sea · Caucasus · Caspian Sea · Tabriz · Kazvin · Mosul · Baghdad · Basra · Rayy · Shiraz · Kerman · PERSIA · Khiva · Merv · Oxus · Nishapur · Balkh · Herat · Ghazni · Samarkand · Indus · Himalayas · Daybul · Muscat · Taima · Khaibar · ARABIA · Red Sea · Zebid · Mocha · Indian Ocean

0 — 500 miles
0 — 800 km

Following the Abbasid conquest in 750, Jerusalem, ruled from Baghdad, declined rapidly in importance and prosperity. This situation worsened still further after the imposition of rule by Egyptian dynasties after 878, when both the Jewish and Christian inhabitants were often subject to persecution.

● Cities ruled by Islam, which contained large Jewish communities.

© Martin Gilbert 1977

Map 7

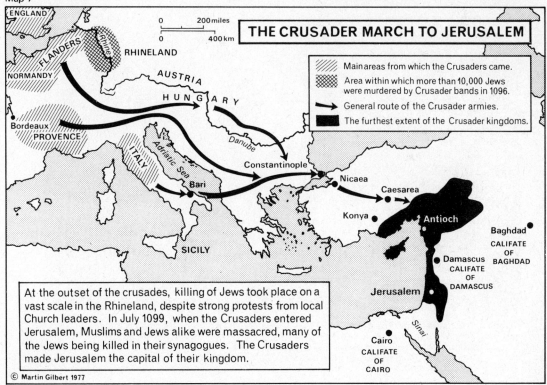

THE CRUSADER MARCH TO JERUSALEM

/// Main areas from which the Crusaders came.

▨ Area within which more than 10,000 Jews were murdered by Crusader bands in 1096.

→ General route of the Crusader armies.

■ The furthest extent of the Crusader kingdoms.

ENGLAND · FLANDERS · NORMANDY · Rhine · RHINELAND · AUSTRIA · HUNGARY · Bordeaux · PROVENCE · ITALY · Adriatic Sea · Danube · Bari · SICILY · Constantinople · Nicaea · Caesarea · Konya · Antioch · Baghdad · CALIFATE OF BAGHDAD · Damascus · CALIFATE OF DAMASCUS · Jerusalem · Sinai · Cairo · CALIFATE OF CAIRO

0 — 200 miles
0 — 400 km

At the outset of the crusades, killing of Jews took place on a vast scale in the Rhineland, despite strong protests from local Church leaders. In July 1099, when the Crusaders entered Jerusalem, Muslims and Jews alike were massacred, many of the Jews being killed in their synagogues. The Crusaders made Jerusalem the capital of their kingdom.

© Martin Gilbert 1977

Map 8

15

Plate 11 One of three hundred tiles brought to Jerusalem from Anatolia in about 1700 AD by Armenian pilgrims. The tiles, intended for the decoration of the Church of the Holy Sepulchre, were in fact used in the Armenian Church of St. James. Only thirty-seven survived in 1922, when the Pro-Jerusalem Society, established by the British authorities, set up a workshop for Armenian Christians to revive the art of ceramic tile-making.

Plate 12 The "Maccabean Pilgrimage" of 1897. A group of British Jews, including the novelist Israel Zangwill (reclining front right), visited Jerusalem in April 1897, four months before the first Zionist Congress met at Basle and advocated the re-establishment of a Jewish State in Palestine. The "Order of Ancient Maccabeans", as it was called, was a charitable society founded in 1896, and made its first land purchase in Palestine in 1914.

JERUSALEM: HOLY CITY, CITY OF PILGRIMAGE SINCE 1000 BC

From the moment of the establishment of the Kingdom of David in 1000BC, and the building of the Temple, Jerusalem became the focal point of Jewish pilgrimage. On each of the three annual pilgrim festivals, Passover, Tabernacles (Succot), and the Feast of Weeks (Shavuot), Jews flocked to the City from the towns and villages of the land of Israel. In the 1,900 years following the destruction of the Temple in 70 AD, Jewish pilgrims continued to make the journey to the City from afar, despite the often enormous difficulties of the journey. Many, on arrival, settled in the City permanently.

In 40 AD the Jewish philosopher, Philo of Alexandria, noted *'Countless multitudes from countless cities come to the Temple at every festival, some by land, and others by sea, from east and west and north and south'*. Twenty-six years later, in 66 AD, the historian Josephus recorded that the Roman Governor of Syria had found the Jewish town of Lydda empty *'for the whole multitude were gone up to Jerusalem to the feast of the Tabernacles'*.

'Whoever goes on a pilgrimage to the Jerusalem sanctuary, and worships there for one and the same year shall be forgiven all his sins'.
SAYINGS OF MOHAMMED

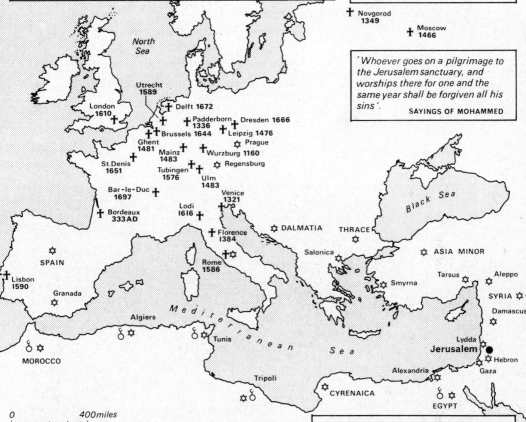

✡ A few of the towns and regions from which Jews went to Jerusalem during the 2,500 years from the Kingdom of David in 1000 BC to 1500 AD. Since 1500 such pilgrimages have continued, until the present day (see PLATE 114).

✝ A few of the towns from which Christian pilgrims went to Jerusalem in the 1,400 years from the Byzantine conquest in 325 AD until 1700 AD. Each of the 21 towns indicated here was one in which at least one book was published by a returning pilgrim or traveller. Between 333 AD and 1500 AD more than 550 books were written by such travellers.

☿ Some of the towns and regions from which Muslims came to Jerusalem after 637AD, many settling permanently in the City.

For the Muslims, after 637 AD, Jerusalem was Al-Bait al-Muquddas (the Holy City), and later Al Quds al-Sharif (the Holy and Noble City), their third holiest city after Mecca and Medina.

© Martin Gilbert 1977

Map 9

17

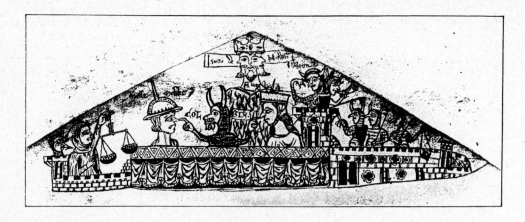

Plate 13 Isaac of Norwich, a Jewish moneylender, depicted in a contemporary cartoon being tortured by the Devil. Isaac was imprisoned by King John in 1210 and his house confiscated. Twenty years earlier, on 16 March 1190, the Jews of York had committed mass suicide rather than submit to the anti-Jewish violence of the mob.

Plate 14 The second expulsion of the Jews from Prague, 1745; from a contemporary print. The Jews of Prague first settled in the city in 906AD. In 1389 more than 3,000 were killed by the mob; in 1421, 1448 and 1483 their ghetto was plundered; in 1541 they were expelled and in 1557 their few remaining houses were burned. Returning in 1638 they were subjected to heavy tax-axtion, and expelled again in 1745. Fifty families were allowed to return in 1748.

JERUSALEM AND THE JEWISH SEARCH FOR A SECURE HAVEN 1000 AD - 1600

| 0 | miles | 400 |
| 0 | km | 500 |

In the six hundred years from 1000 AD to 1600, Jews were frequently expelled, often in circumstances of great brutality, from many of the States and cities of Christian Europe. Many sought refuge in Muslim North Africa (where they had to accept the status of second-class citizens), in eastern Europe (where further persecution and restrictions were not infrequent), and under the somewhat more tolerant rule of the Ottoman Turks, who had driven the Mamluks from Jerusalem in 1517, and whose Empire extended by 1600 from the Caucasus to Algiers.

Some of the countries from which the Jews were expelled, at different times between 1012 AD and 1495.

Some of the towns from which the Jews were expelled, at different times between 1010 AD and 1540.

----→ Journey of the Italian rabbi, Obadiah di Bertinora, between 1485 and 1488, going to settle in Jerusalem.

LITHUANIA 1495

Atlantic Ocean

North Sea

Baltic Sea

York

Vilna □   □ Minsk
□ Grodno
Berlin 1349   □ Gomel
Norwich
Posen   Pinsk □   □ Chernigov   □ Kharkov
ENGLAND AND WALES 1290
Cologne 1096   Cracow 1494   Zhitomir □ □ Kiev
Radom
Mainz 1012   Gotha 1212   Prague 1541   Beltsy ●
Paris 1394
Lyons 1420   Berne 1259   Vienna 1349   Kishinev ●
Udine   Budapest 1360   Akkerman ●   CRIMEA 1016
PORTUGAL 1497
Toulouse 1420   Turin □   Venice   Braila ●
Spalato   Nicopolis ●
SPAIN 1492   PROVENCE 1394   Livorno   Cattaro   Black Sea
Rome   Genoa 1550   Adriatic Sea   Adrianople   Constantinople
SICILY 1492   KINGDOM OF NAPLES   Salonika ●   Bursa ●
Chanak ●   Aleppo ●
Fez □ □ Oran   Algiers ●   Tunis ●   Smyrna ●   Tripoli ●
Tlemcen   SICILY 1495   RHODES 1502   Damascus ● Safed ●
MALTA 1492   Mediterranean Sea   Tiberias ●
NORTH   AFRICA   Tripoli ●   Alexandria ●   Jerusalem Hebron
Caucasus
Cairo
EGYPT   Red Sea

Throughout 600 years of European persecution, small numbers of Jews always sought to settle in Jerusalem, despite the great distances involved, the hardships of the journey, and the uncertainty of a friendly welcome by the ruling power. During the sixteenth century four synagogues were built in Jerusalem to accommodate the growing Jewish population. By 1700 there were an estimated 300 Jewish families, totalling about 1,200 persons. But no century was entirely free from problems: thus in 1586 the Ottoman ruler, or Kadi, deprived the community of the use of its synagogues; in 1726 local Muslim Arabs seized another synagogue (which they held until 1816) and burnt the scrolls of the law.

□ Some of the towns in North Africa, Italy, Dalmatia, Poland and the Ukraine in which many Jews found refuge.

● Some of the towns in the Ottoman Empire in which the Jews found refuge after 1517.

The boundaries of the Ottoman Empire by 1600.

© Martin Gilbert 1977

Map 10

19

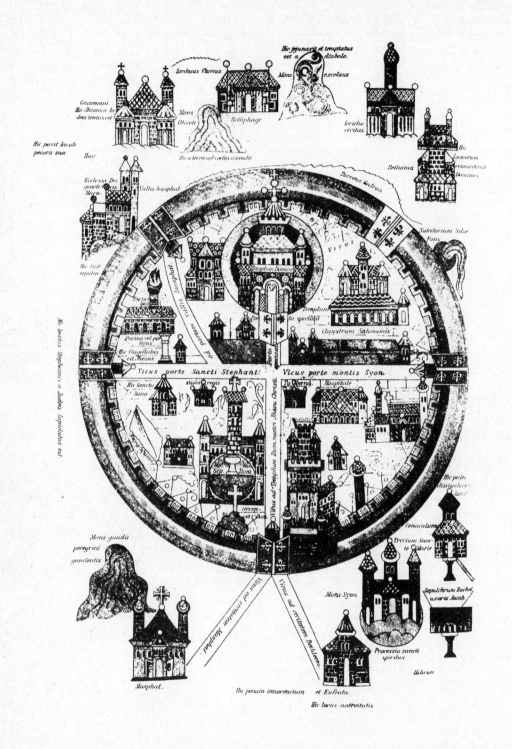

Plate 15   A map of Jerusalem in the twelfth century. On the Dome of the Rock, renamed "Templum Domini", the Cross has replaced the Crescent.

CRUSADER JERUSALEM

Once Jerusalem had been conquered by the Crusaders, as many as 10,000 Christian pilgrims made the journey every year, some from as far away as Scandinavia, Muscovy and Portugal; and each year a small number of these pilgrims decided to remain permanently in the city.

Following the Crusader entry into Jerusalem in 1099, all the Jews in the City were either murdered, sold into slavery in Europe, or ransomed to the Jewish community of Egypt. The Crusaders then brought Christian Arab tribes from east of the river Jordan, and settled them in the former Jewish Quarter, between St. Stephen's Gate and the Gate of Jehoshafat.

■ Principal Crusader buildings.

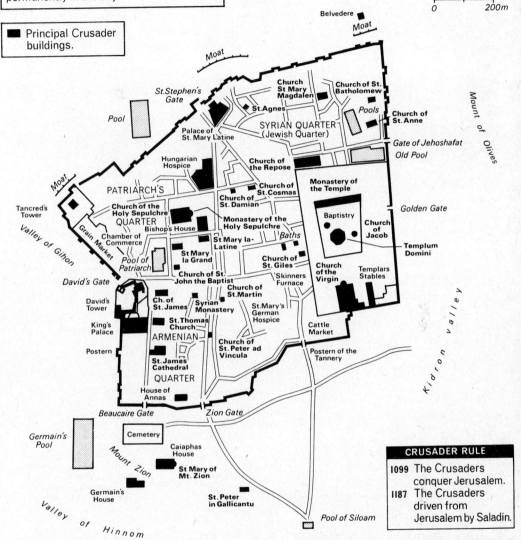

0   200 yards
0   200m

CRUSADER RULE

1099 The Crusaders conquer Jerusalem.
1187 The Crusaders driven from Jerusalem by Saladin.

Even Crusader rule did not deter one Jew from trying to settle in Jerusalem, for in 1140 the Spanish-born poet and philosopher Judah Halevi set out for Jerusalem via Cairo. According to legend, he was approaching the City Walls when an Arab horseman, leaving by one of the Gates, trampled him to death. As he lay dying he is said to have recited one of his own poems: "Zion, shall I not seek thee".

'Beautiful heights, joy of the world, city of a great king. For you my soul yearns from the lands of the west.
My pity collects and is roused when I remember the past. Your story in exile, and your Temple destroyed....
I shall cherish your stones and kiss them. And your earth will be sweeter than honey to my taste'.
JUDAH HALEVI
c. 1140

© Martin Gilbert 1977

Map 11

21

Plate 16　A Jewish family in their house on Mount Zion. An engraving published by W.H. Bartlett in 1844. Describing the head of the family, said to be "the wealthiest Jew in Jerusalem", Bartlett wrote: "His career is remarkable; in his youth he had been a wanderer under the burning tropics, as well as in England and in Spain, and by various means having accumulated a sum sufficient to render him the envy of his poor abject brethren, he repaired to the city of his fathers."

Plate 17　Sir Moses and Lady Montefiore entering Jerusalem in 1839; a sketch from Montefiore's album. Born in 1784, Montefiore retired from business as a London stockbroker in 1824, and first visited Palestine three years later. A noted philanthropist, he died at the age of 100 having made seven visits to Jerusalem. He initiated several works of charity and of Jewish self-improvement in Jerusalem, including the Jewish Hospital (see Plate 31) and the "Montefiore Houses" for poor Jews (see Plate 33).

THE RETURN OF THE JEWS TO JERUSALEM 1200 - 1841

In 1210, following the defeat of the Crusaders, groups of Jews began to return to Jerusalem. Henceforth, without interruption, and in every decade, individual Jews, and groups of Jews, reached the city from Europe and the Mahgreb, forming an ever-growing community. Driven out by the Tartar invasion of 1244, they had returned by 1250. Three times a day the Jews repeated in their prayers: "And to Jerusalem Thy city mayest thou return in mercy, and dwell in its midst as Thou hast spoken, and rebuild it soon, in our days, for evermore....."

■ Areas from which some 300 Rabbis travelled to Jerusalem, Acre and Ramla in 1210 AD, to strengthen the Jewish communities weakened by the Crusader massacres and expulsions.

⊙ Some of the regions, and a few of the towns, from which individual Jews are known to have travelled to Jerusalem after 1267, settling permanently, and whose families formed, by 1841, the largest single community in Jerusalem itself.

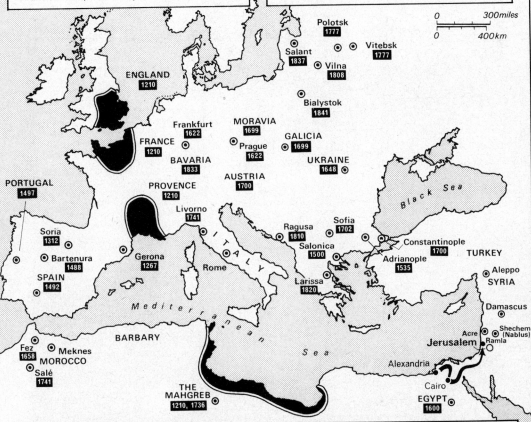

'What shall I say of this land? Great is its desolation. The more holy the place, the greater the desolation. Jerusalem is the most desolate of all.... The only Jewish residents are two brothers, dyers by trade. There the ten men meet (for prayer) and on Sabbath hold service at their house..... The city has no master, and he that wishes may take possession of the ruins. We have procured, from Shechem, Scrolls of the Law, which had been carried thither from Jerusalem at the time of the Tartar invasion. Thus we shall organize a synagogue, and shall be able to pray here. Men flock from Damascus, Aleppo, and from all parts to Jerusalem to behold the Place of the Sanctuary, and to mourn over it. May you, my son and your brothers, and the whole of our family, see the salvation of Jerusalem'.

NAHMANIDES, LETTER TO HIS SON, 1267

↗ Napoleon's march from Egypt to Acre, where he was defeated by the British in 1799. According to his official newspaper, the 'Moniteur', one of his aims was 'to give back to the Jews their Jerusalem' ('pour rendre aux juifs leur Jérusalem').

'Bonaparte has caused a proclamation to be issued, in which he invites all the Jews of Asia and Africa to come and range themselves under his flags, in order to re-establish Jerusalem as of old'.

REPORT IN THE 'MONITEUR' 1799

© Martin Gilbert 1977

Map 12

23

Plate 18 The Damascus Gate; a photograph taken in 1896. One of the main entrances to Jerusalem from Roman times, this, the present gate, was built by Sultan Suleiman in 1537. The pinnacles on the Gate, which had almost entirely disintegrated by 1917 as a result of Ottoman neglect, were restored to Sultan Suleiman's original plan in 1921, by the British Mandate Department of Antiquities.

Plate 19 The Jaffa Gate; a photograph taken in about 1914. The clock tower, built by the Turks in 1907, was removed by the British Mandate authorities in 1924. Both the roofed building on the left of the entrance, and the Ottoman fountain (with dome) on the right, were also demolished by the British during the Mandate period. Bottom right — a corner of the coffee shop, also shown on the front cover (see PLATE 1).

MAMLUK AND OTTOMAN JERUSALEM

0   yards   300

0   metres   200

Following the final defeat of the Crusaders in 1244, Muslim rule returned to Jerusalem, first under the Mamluks of Egypt (1250 - 1517), and then under the Ottoman Turks (1517 - 1917). Both Christians and Jews were subjected to continual indignities: a tannery was built next to the Church of the Holy Sepulchre, and a slaughterhouse next to the Ben Zakkai synagogue 'so that an evil smell should ever plague the infidels'.

The City walls, as restored and strengthened by Sultan Suleiman between 1539 and 1542.

■ Principal buildings constructed during Mamluk rule.

▨ Principal buildings constructed between 1517 and 1840, during the first 500 years of Ottoman rule.

The Via Dolorosa, centre of Christian pilgrimage.

City Gates: Mamluk names in italics, Ottoman names in white
i.e. *Jaffa Gate*

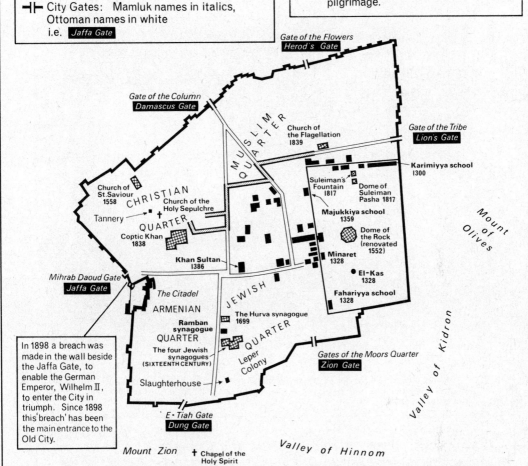

Gate of the Flowers
Herod's Gate

Gate of the Column
Damascus Gate

MUSLIM QUARTER

Church of the Flagellation 1839

Gate of the Tribe
Lion's Gate

Karimiyya school 1300

Suleiman's Fountain 1817

Dome of Suleiman Pasha 1817

Majukkiya school 1359

Church of St.Saviour 1558

CHRISTIAN

Church of the Holy Sepulchre

Tannery

QUARTER

Coptic Khan 1838

Khan Sultan 1386

Dome of the Rock (renovated 1552)

Minaret 1328

● El-Kas 1328

Fahariyya school 1328

Mihrab Daoud Gate
Jaffa Gate

The Citadel

ARMENIAN

Ramban synagogue

QUARTER

The four Jewish synagogues (SIXTEENTH CENTURY)

JEWISH QUARTER

The Hurva synagogue 1699

Leper Colony

Gates of the Moors Quarter
Zion Gate

Mount of Olives

In 1898 a breach was made in the wall beside the Jaffa Gate, to enable the German Emperor, Wilhelm II, to enter the City in triumph. Since 1898 this 'breach' has been the main entrance to the Old City.

Slaughterhouse

E - Tiah Gate
Dung Gate

Valley of Kidron

Mount Zion   ✝ Chapel of the Holy Spirit

Valley of Hinnom

1244 The Kharezmian Tartars sack Jerusalem, massacring the Christians, and killing many Jews. Some Jews escaped to Nablus, and settled there.

1368 Muslims murder twelve monks on Mount Zion, and harrass those who remain.

1428 When German Jews try to buy a site for worship on Mount Zion, the Christians of the City protest to the Pope, who asked the Italian republics not to take any Jews on board ships going to the Holy Land.

1440 Mamluks impose a heavy annual tax on all Jews. Many Jewish craftsmen, who could not afford to pay, forced to leave the City.

1460 Muslims destroy the Chapel of the Holy Spirit on Mount Zion.

1551 Franciscans driven from their Church on Mount Zion.

1775 Ottoman Turks impose a head-tax on all Jews.

1780 Monks of the Monastery of the Cross massacred by Arab marauders.

© Martin Gilbert 1977

Map 13

Plate 20 "A Jewish Cotton-Cleaner, separating seeds from cotton by the ancient process of bowing it".
Both the picture and the caption are from Colonel Wilson's *Picturesque Palestine,* published
in London in 1878.

"Here, then, among the ruins of Zion, still lingers a remnant of the
chosen people— but how changed their circumstances! Instead of the
'mighty man, and the man of war, the judge, and the prophet, and the
prudent, and the ancient, the captain of fifty, and the honourable man,
and the counsellor, and the cunning artificier, and the eloquent orator,'
we see a despised body, chiefly of exiles, crouching under general
dislike and persecution; yet with inflexible tenacity clinging to the spot
which recalls their past greatness, and inspires visionary hopes of future
domination."

W.H. BARTLETT, 1844

THE JEWS OF JERUSALEM UNDER OTTOMAN RULE 1517-1831

⊙) Towns and regions to which
■ Jerusalem Jews are known to
have travelled in search of alms,
or as teachers and scholars.

• Towns from which Jews
frequently moved to Jerusalem,
or in which Jews from Jerusalem
often settled.

During the seventeenth and eighteenth centuries, many Jerusalem Jews, scholars and rabbis, travelled from Jerusalem to teach in Jewish communities elsewhere, and also to seek alms and charity for the poorer members of their own community. There was also a regular movement of families, in both directions, between Jerusalem and several towns of the eastern Mediterranean region.

THE JEWISH COMMUNITY IN JERUSALEM

1586 Turks refuse Jews use of the Ramban synagogue.

1625 Under harsh taxation of Ibn Faruk, Jerusalem's Jews seek alms throughout eastern Europe.

1720 Arabs seize the Ashkenazi synagogue, and burn the scrolls of the Law. The synagogue was not returned to the Jewish community until 1816.

1787 The roof of another synagogue falls in under a heavy weight of snow. The Turks refuse for several years to allow the roof to be repaired.

1812 Jews flee from Safed to Jerusalem, following an epidemic.

© Martin Gilbert 1977

'The greatest part of the Jews here are poor, as they have no opportunity of trafficking; for without it they cannot thrive in any part of the world. They have no other income here than they can get from the Pilgrims of their nation, who come far and wide from all places to pay their respects to the seat of their forefathers. Their Rabbi has large revenues from his brethren throughout the whole world, of which the Turks draw the greatest part; for Jews as well as Christians must constantly bring offerings to their altars, if they will kiss their holy places in peace'. HASSELQUIST, 'VOYAGES AND TRAVELS' 1766

Map 14

27

Ierusalem as it now is

1 Chriſt's Sepulchre. 2. David's Houſe.. 3 Dives's Houſe. 4. The Virgin Mary's Houſe.

Plate 21 A map of Jerusalem, from Nath Crouch's book *Two Journeys to Jerusalem,* published in London in 1719. Crouch was an English Christian pilgrim, who visited the City in 1669.

'Jerusalem is the centre around which the Jew builds in airy dreams the mansions of his future greatness. Thither he returns from Spain, Portugal, Germany, Barbary, etc., after all his toilings and all his struggles up the steps of life, to walk the streets of his own happy Zion.'

HANMER DUPUIS 'THE HOLY PLACES' 1856

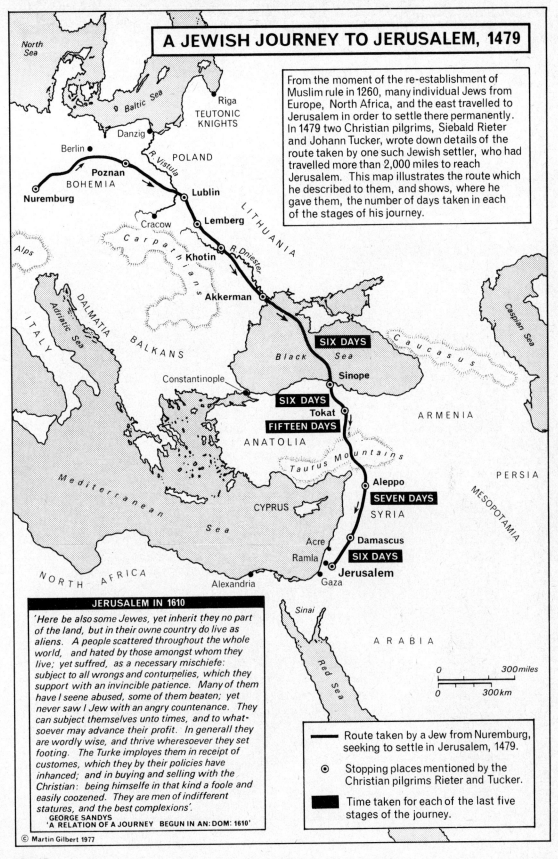

A JEWISH JOURNEY TO JERUSALEM, 1479

From the moment of the re-establishment of Muslim rule in 1260, many individual Jews from Europe, North Africa, and the east travelled to Jerusalem in order to settle there permanently. In 1479 two Christian pilgrims, Siebald Rieter and Johann Tucker, wrote down details of the route taken by one such Jewish settler, who had travelled more than 2,000 miles to reach Jerusalem. This map illustrates the route which he described to them, and shows, where he gave them, the number of days taken in each of the stages of his journey.

North Sea

Riga
TEUTONIC KNIGHTS
Baltic Sea
Danzig
Berlin
POLAND
R. Vistula
Poznan
BOHEMIA
Nuremburg
Lublin
Cracow
Lemberg
LITHUANIA
Carpathians
Khotin
R. Dniester
Akkerman
Alps
ITALY
Adriatic Sea
DALMATIA
BALKANS
SIX DAYS
Black Sea
Caucasus
Caspian Sea
Constantinople
Sinope
SIX DAYS
Tokat
ARMENIA
FIFTEEN DAYS
ANATOLIA
Taurus Mountains
PERSIA
MESOPOTAMIA
Mediterranean Sea
CYPRUS
Aleppo
SEVEN DAYS
SYRIA
Acre
Damascus
Ramla
SIX DAYS
Jerusalem
Gaza
NORTH AFRICA
Alexandria
Sinai
ARABIA
Red Sea

0 — 300 miles
0 — 300 km

⎯⎯⎯ Route taken by a Jew from Nuremburg, seeking to settle in Jerusalem, 1479.

⊙ Stopping places mentioned by the Christian pilgrims Rieter and Tucker.

▬ Time taken for each of the last five stages of the journey.

JERUSALEM IN 1610

'Here be also some Jewes, yet inherit they no part of the land, but in their owne country do live as aliens. A people scattered throughout the whole world, and hated by those amongst whom they live; yet suffred, as a necessary mischiefe: subject to all wrongs and contumelies, which they support with an invincible patience. Many of them have I seene abused, some of them beaten; yet never saw I Jew with an angry countenance. They can subject themselves unto times, and to what-soever may advance their profit. In generall they are wordly wise, and thrive wheresoever they set footing. The Turke imployes them in receipt of customes, which they by their policies have inhanced; and in buying and selling with the Christian: being himselfe in that kind a foole and easily coozened. They are men of indifferent statures, and the best complexions'.
GEORGE SANDYS
'A RELATION OF A JOURNEY BEGUN IN AN: DOM: 1610'

© Martin Gilbert 1977

Map 15

29

Plate 22 The Wailing Wall in 1894, photographed by Robert Bain.

Plate 23 The Wailing Wall in 1912, photographed during a visit by residents of the Jerusalem Old Men's Home.

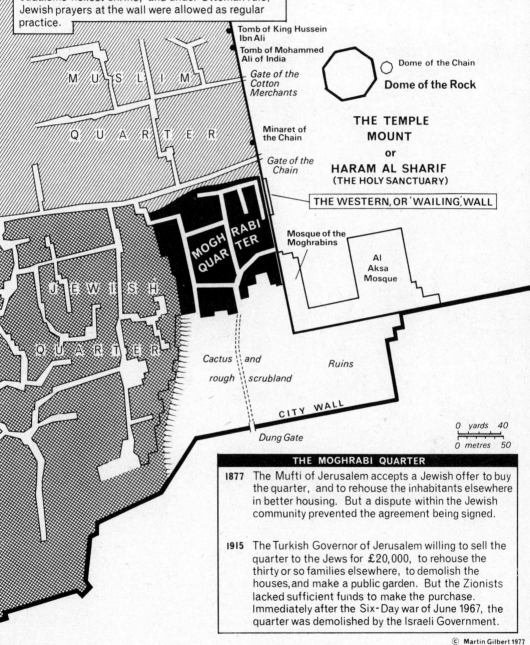

THE 'WAILING WALL' UNDER OTTOMAN RULE 1517 - 1917

Following the destruction of the Temple by the Romans, Jews continued to visit that section of the western wall of the Temple Mount which remained intact and exposed, to lament the destruction of the Temple, and to pray for it to be rebuilt. A synagogue was constructed at the wall shortly before the Crusader period. With the return of the Jews to the City after the Crusades, the western wall served as Judaism's holiest shrine, and under Ottoman rule, Jewish prayers at the wall were allowed as regular practice.

'The Jews of Jerusalem have obtained permission to assemble on this spot to lament over the desolation of their people, and to implore the restoration of the scene of their former glory, chanting in mournful melody, not unmingled with a dawn of hope:
  "Lord, build - Lord build -
   Build Thy house speedily.
   In haste! in haste! Even in our days,
   Build Thy house speedily ".'

W.H. BARTLETT
1851

Tomb of King Hussein Ibn Ali

Tomb of Mohammed Ali of India

Gate of the Cotton Merchants

Dome of the Chain

Dome of the Rock

MUSLIM QUARTER

Minaret of the Chain

Gate of the Chain

THE TEMPLE MOUNT
or
HARAM AL SHARIF
(THE HOLY SANCTUARY)

THE WESTERN, OR 'WAILING' WALL

MOGHRABI QUARTER

Mosque of the Moghrabins

Al Aksa Mosque

JEWISH QUARTER

Cactus and rough scrubland

Ruins

CITY WALL

Dung Gate

0 yards 40
0 metres 50

THE MOGHRABI QUARTER

1877 The Mufti of Jerusalem accepts a Jewish offer to buy the quarter, and to rehouse the inhabitants elsewhere in better housing. But a dispute within the Jewish community prevented the agreement being signed.

1915 The Turkish Governor of Jerusalem willing to sell the quarter to the Jews for £20,000, to rehouse the thirty or so families elsewhere, to demolish the houses, and make a public garden. But the Zionists lacked sufficient funds to make the purchase. Immediately after the Six-Day war of June 1967, the quarter was demolished by the Israeli Government.

© Martin Gilbert 1977

Map 16

31

Plate 24   A portrait of Sabbatai Zevi, sketched by an eye-witness in Syria, and first published in Amsterdam in 1669. Zevi had passed through Aleppo in 1665, when he told the rabbi there, Solomon Laniado (as Laniado wrote to two rabbis in Kurdistan) of God's words to him: "Thou art the saviour of Israel, the messiah, the son of David, the annointed of the God of Jacob, and thou art destined to redeem Israel, to gather it from the four corners of the earth to Jerusalem". Zevi's movement gained great impetus from the Chmielnicki massacres in the Ukraine, when more than 100,000 Jews were murdered in cold blood.

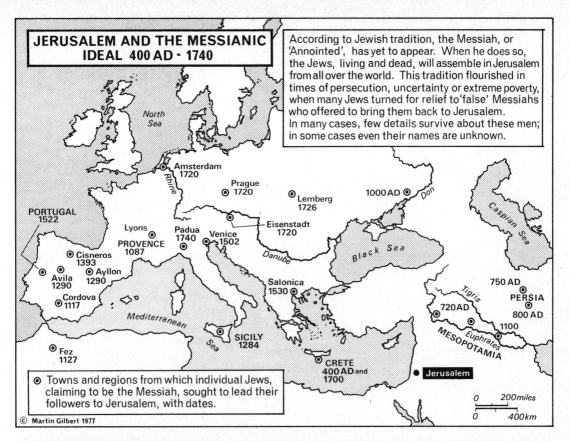

JERUSALEM AND THE MESSIANIC IDEAL 400 AD - 1740

According to Jewish tradition, the Messiah, or 'Annointed', has yet to appear. When he does so, the Jews, living and dead, will assemble in Jerusalem from all over the world. This tradition flourished in times of persecution, uncertainty or extreme poverty, when many Jews turned for relief to 'false' Messiahs who offered to bring them back to Jerusalem.

In many cases, few details survive about these men; in some cases even their names are unknown.

North Sea

Amsterdam 1720

Prague 1720

Lemberg 1726

1000 AD

Don

Caspian Sea

PORTUGAL 1522

Lyons

Padua 1740

Venice 1502

Eisenstadt 1720

Danube

Black Sea

PROVENCE 1087

Cisneros 1393

Avila 1290

Ayllon 1290

Salonica 1530

750 AD

720 AD

Tigris

PERSIA

800 AD

1100

Cordova 1117

Mediterranean Sea

SICILY 1284

Euphrates

MESOPOTAMIA

Fez 1127

CRETE 400 AD and 1700

● Jerusalem

⊙ Towns and regions from which individual Jews, claiming to be the Messiah, sought to lead their followers to Jerusalem, with dates.

0   200 miles

0   400 km

© Martin Gilbert 1977

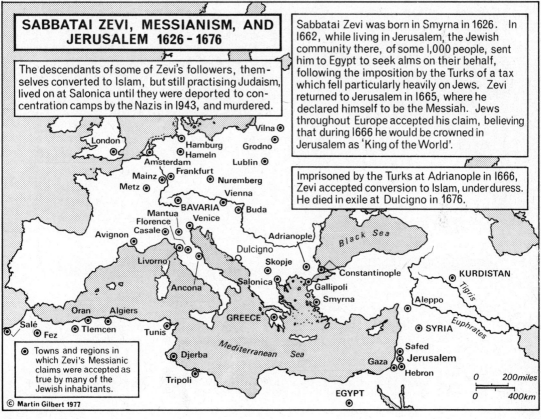

SABBATAI ZEVI, MESSIANISM, AND JERUSALEM 1626 - 1676

The descendants of some of Zevi's followers, themselves converted to Islam, but still practising Judaism, lived on at Salonica until they were deported to concentration camps by the Nazis in 1943, and murdered.

Sabbatai Zevi was born in Smyrna in 1626. In 1662, while living in Jerusalem, the Jewish community there, of some 1,000 people, sent him to Egypt to seek alms on their behalf, following the imposition by the Turks of a tax which fell particularly heavily on Jews. Zevi returned to Jerusalem in 1665, where he declared himself to be the Messiah. Jews throughout Europe accepted his claim, believing that during 1666 he would be crowned in Jerusalem as 'King of the World'.

Imprisoned by the Turks at Adrianople in 1666, Zevi accepted conversion to Islam, under duress. He died in exile at Dulcigno in 1676.

Vilna

London

Hamburg

Hameln

Grodno

Amsterdam

Lublin

Mainz

Frankfurt

Nuremberg

Metz

Vienna

BAVARIA

Buda

Mantua

Venice

Florence

Casale

Avignon

Adrianople

Black Sea

Dulcigno

Livorno

Skopje

Constantinople

KURDISTAN

Ancona

Salonica

Gallipoli

Aleppo

Smyrna

Oran

Algiers

GREECE

Tigris

Salé

Tlemcen

Tunis

SYRIA

Fez

Euphrates

Mediterranean Sea

Safed

Djerba

Gaza

Jerusalem

Hebron

Tripoli

0   200 miles

⊙ Towns and regions in which Zevi's Messianic claims were accepted as true by many of the Jewish inhabitants.

EGYPT

0   400 km

© Martin Gilbert 1977

Map 18

33

SEPVLCRO DE CHRISTO

SOPRA QVESTA PIETRA CASCO CHRISTO PORTANTE ✝

Plate 25 The Church of the Holy Sepulchre, one of the prints in Michiel Miloco's pilgrim Guide. The
Church's history had been a troubled one: built by St Helena in 333AD, it was destroyed by
the Persians in 614, restored a few years later by Modestus, burned by Ikshhid, a Turkish ruler
of Egypt, in 934; burned by the Fatimites in 969; demolished by the Druse leader El Hakim Bi
Amr Allah in 1010, restored by Michael IV in 1037, and by Constantine Monomach in 1048,
pillaged by the Seljuk Turks in 1077, in part reconstructed by the Crusaders from 1140 to 1149,
severely damaged during the Kharismian invasion of 1244. Again rebuilt in 1719, it was in such
urgent need of restoration that it had to be in part reconstructed. Then, in 1808, it was almost
entirely destroyed by fire, being rebuilt once more in 1810.

A CHRISTIAN PILGRIMAGE OF 1670

——— A pilgrim route to Jerusalem, as described in a pilgrim Guide of 1670, published in Venice by Michiel Miloco.

– – – Journeys beyond Jerusalem, as described in the Guide.

• Places visited en route to Jerusalem, and beyond it.

▬ Places to be visited during the course of the pilgrims' travels in the Holy Land.

◉ The Capital city of the Ottoman Empire, 1517-1920.

With the establishment of Ottoman rule in 1517, Christian pilgrimages to Jerusalem increased in frequency. At Easter, pilgrims were said to double the City's population. This map illustrates a pilgrimage from Venice in 1670.

'Jerusalem is inhabited by some Christians, (who make a great benefit of shewing the Sepulchre of Christ) and of Late Years also by Moors, Arabians, Greeks, Latines, Turks, Jews; nay, I may say, with People of all Nations'.
NATH CROUCH, AN ENGLISH PILGRIM WRITING IN 1719.

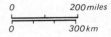

'And having heard by some means or other in times past, very much discourse of the beauty and the pleasant situation of that City; of the sweet temper of the inhabitants, and the many goodly things that were to be seen and enjoyed there; he was instantly prepossessed with a strong desire to remove his feet thither.
When he did eat or drink Jerusalem would still be in his mouth, when he was in Company, Jerusalem stole away his heart from him; Nay, in his very sleep it would stay away, but he was wont to dream fine things of Jerusalem'. **AN ENGLISH PILGRIM, WRITING IN 1684**

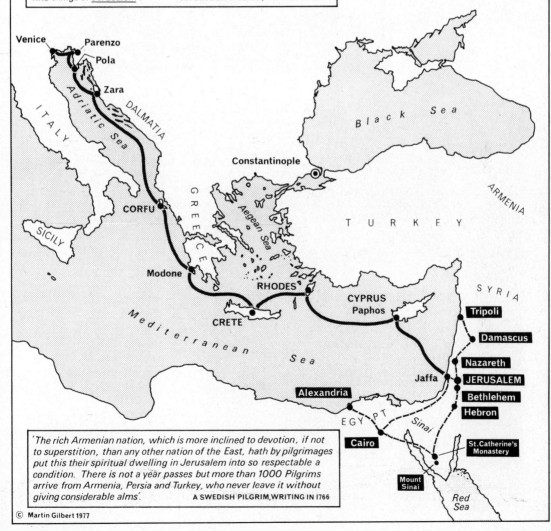

'The rich Armenian nation, which is more inclined to devotion, if not to superstition, than any other nation of the East, hath by pilgrimages put this their spiritual dwelling in Jerusalem into so respectable a condition. There is not a year passes but more than 1000 Pilgrims arrive from Armenia, Persia and Turkey, who never leave it without giving considerable alms'. **A SWEDISH PILGRIM, WRITING IN 1766**

© Martin Gilbert 1977

Map 19

35

TELESCOPIC PEEP AT THE HARAM

Plate 26 A "Telescopic Peep at the Haram"; an engraving of 1855, done at a time when no Christians were allowed to set foot in the Haram enclosure.

Plate 27 The Ecce Homo Arch, on the Via Dolorosa. One of the first photographs of Jerusalem, taken by Auguste Salzman, and published by him in Paris in 1856.

JERUSALEM 1830-1850

1831 Jerusalem captured by Mohammed Ali of Egypt.
1836 Ibrahim Pasha allows the Jews to repair their four main synagogues.
1840 Ottoman Turkish rule restored, but many Muslims from Egypt settle permanently in the City.
1842 The London Society for Promoting Christianity among the Jews sends a physician.
1843 A Jewish physician arrives, to relieve Jews of dependence upon the London Society physician.

'A large number of houses in Jerusalem are in a dilapidated and ruinous state. Nobody seems to make repairs so long as his dwelling does not absolutely refuse him shelter and safety. If one room tumbles about his ears, he removes into another, and permits rubbish and vermin to accumulate as they will in the deserted halls'.
DR. JOHN KITTO
'MODERN JERUSALEM' 1847

MUSLIM QUARTER

'in the N.E. the whole slope within the city walls is occupied by gardens, fields, and olive yards, with comparatively few houses or ruined dwellings; the whole being more the aspect of a village in the country than of a quarter in a city'.
E. ROBINSON AND E. SMITH,
'BIBLICAL RESEARCHES' 1838

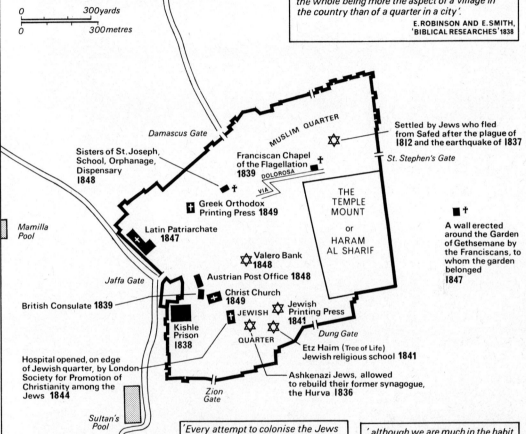

0 ———— 300 yards
0 ———— 300 metres

Damascus Gate

MUSLIM QUARTER

Settled by Jews who fled from Safed after the plague of 1812 and the earthquake of 1837

St. Stephen's Gate

Sisters of St. Joseph, School, Orphanage, Dispensary **1848**

Franciscan Chapel of the Flagellation **1839**
VIA DOLOROSA

Greek Orthodox Printing Press **1849**

THE TEMPLE MOUNT or HARAM AL SHARIF

Mamilla Pool

Latin Patriarchate **1847**

Valero Bank **1848**

Austrian Post Office **1848**

A wall erected around the Garden of Gethsemane by the Franciscans, to whom the garden belonged **1847**

Jaffa Gate

Christ Church **1849**

British Consulate **1839**

JEWISH

Jewish Printing Press **1841**

Kishle Prison **1838**

QUARTER

Dung Gate

Etz Haim (Tree of Life) Jewish religious school **1841**

Hospital opened, on edge of Jewish quarter, by London Society for Promotion of Christianity among the Jews **1844**

Zion Gate

Ashkenazi Jews, allowed to rebuild their former synagogue, the Hurva **1836**

Sultan's Pool

'Every attempt to colonise the Jews in other countries has failed – their eye has steadily rested on their beloved Jerusalem'.
JUDGE NOAH 'VOICE OF JACOB' OCTOBER 1844

' although we are much in the habit of regarding Jerusalem as a Moslem city, the Moslems do not actually constitute more than one-third of the entire population'.
DR. JOHN KITTO
'MODERN JERUSALEM' 1847

JEWISH QUARTER

' what a painful change has passed over the circumstances and condition of the poor Jew that in his own city, and close by where his temple stood, he has to suffer oppression and persecution. In Jerusalem his case is a very hard one, for if he should have a little of this world's goods in his possession, he is oppressed and robbed by the Turks in a most unmerciful manner; in short, for him there is neither law nor justice'.
JOHN LOTHIAN
4 DECEMBER 1843

'The influx of Jews has been very considerable of late. A fortnight since 150 arrived here from Algiers. There is now a large number of Jews here from the coast of Africa, who are about to form themselves into a separate congregation'.
REV. F.C. EWALD
LETTER FOR 'JEWISH INTELLIGENCE'
30 NOVEMBER 1843

POPULATION ESTIMATE, 1845 OF DR. SCHULTZE, PRUSSIAN CONSUL

Jews	7,120
Muslims	5,000
Christians	3,390
Turkish Soldiers	800
Europeans	100
TOTAL POPULATION	**16,410**

© Martin Gilbert 1977

Map 20

37

Plate 28   The City from the Mount of Olives, engraved by E. Brandard.

Plate 29   The Citadel from the south, engraved by R. Wallis

A CHRISTIAN VISITOR OF 1842

In the summer of 1842 a British traveller, W.H.Bartlett, visited Jerusalem, with the aim of publishing 'a clear, connected and accurate view' of the City. This map, based on Bartlett's own sketch, is accompanied by quotations from his book 'Walks About the City and Environs of Jerusalem', published in 1843, and is illustrated by two drawings from that volume.

'If the traveller can forget that he is treading on the grave of a people from whom his religion has sprung, on the dust of her kings, prophets, and holy men, there is certainly no city in the world that he will sooner wish to leave than Jerusalem. Nothing can be more void of interest than her gloomy, half-ruinous streets and poverty stricken bazaars, which, except at the period of the pilgrimage at Easter, present no signs of life or study of character to the observer'.

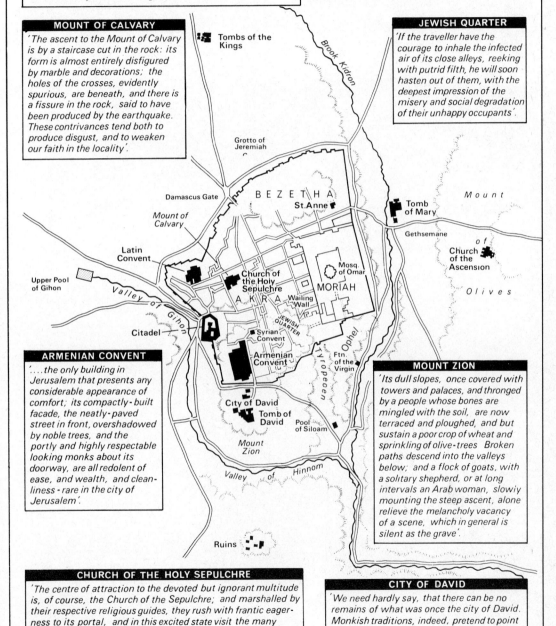

MOUNT OF CALVARY

'The ascent to the Mount of Calvary is by a staircase cut in the rock: its form is almost entirely disfigured by marble and decorations; the holes of the crosses, evidently spurious, are beneath, and there is a fissure in the rock, said to have been produced by the earthquake. These contrivances tend both to produce disgust, and to weaken our faith in the locality'.

JEWISH QUARTER

'If the traveller have the courage to inhale the infected air of its close alleys, reeking with putrid filth, he will soon hasten out of them, with the deepest impression of the misery and social degradation of their unhappy occupants'.

ARMENIAN CONVENT

'....the only building in Jerusalem that presents any considerable appearance of comfort; its compactly-built facade, the neatly-paved street in front, overshadowed by noble trees, and the portly and highly respectable looking monks about its doorway, are all redolent of ease, and wealth, and cleanliness - rare in the city of Jerusalem'.

MOUNT ZION

'Its dull slopes, once covered with towers and palaces, and thronged by a people whose bones are mingled with the soil, are now terraced and ploughed, and but sustain a poor crop of wheat and sprinkling of olive-trees Broken paths descend into the valleys below; and a flock of goats, with a solitary shepherd, or at long intervals an Arab woman, slowly mounting the steep ascent, alone relieve the melancholy vacancy of a scene, which in general is silent as the grave'.

CHURCH OF THE HOLY SEPULCHRE

'The centre of attraction to the devoted but ignorant multitude is, of course, the Church of the Sepulchre; and marshalled by their respective religious guides, they rush with frantic eagerness to its portal, and in this excited state visit the many stations invented or imagined in credulous ages. The whole scene of Christ's crucifixion and entombment are before the eye with such vividness, that even Protestants who come to scoff, have hardly been able to resist the contagious effect of sympathy'.

CITY OF DAVID

'We need hardly say, that there can be no remains of what was once the city of David. Monkish traditions, indeed, pretend to point out some, but they are wholly destitute of foundation; a vast accumulation of debris, from thirty to forty feet in depth, has buried every fragment of it'.

Map labels: Tombs of the Kings; Brook Kidron; Grotto of Jeremiah; Damascus Gate; BEZETHA; St.Anne; Tomb of Mary; Mount of Calvary; Gethsemane; Mount; Church of the Ascension; Olives; Latin Convent; Mosq. of Omar; MORIAH; Upper Pool of Gihon; Church of the Holy Sepulchre; AKRA; Wailing Wall; JEWISH QUARTER; Valley of Gihon; Syrian Convent; Citadel; Armenian Convent; Ftn. of the Virgin; Ophel; Tyropoeon; City of David; Tomb of David; Pool of Siloam; Mount Zion; Valley of Hinnom; Ruins

Map 21

Plate 30 Jewish workers at Abraham's Vineyard preparing stones for a building; a photograph taken in 1906.

JEWISH HOSPITAL.

Plate 31 The Jewish hospital, from a print published in 1855.

JERUSALEM IN THE 1850s

ABRAHAM'S VINEYARD

'On one occassion I witnessed about forty Jews engaged in clearing a field, which had been purchased, or leased, by some society at home, and these Jews were employed to work the land by the English Consul, in order to afford some relief, however partial, to their exigencies. They appeared very thankful, and willing to work for the trifling wages given them. A more interesting sight, among sights in Palestine, could not have been witnessed, than once more to behold these people working and tilling that land which ratified the covenant between God and man: this was a revival of field labour after the lapse of so many ages marked by destruction, dispersion, and desolation of every kind'.

HANMER DUPUIS 1856

HARAM

'This area, formerly the most holy place of the Jews, is now deemed the most holy place of the Mohommedans, and no Christian foot is allowed to enter its precincts'.

W.H.BARTLETT
'A PILGRIMAGE THROUGH THE HOLY LAND'
1851

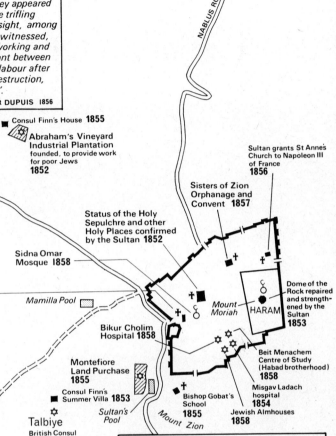

```
0          500 yards
0          500 metres
```

Lifta **1855**

† ■   ■ Ludwig Schneller's house (deserted because of bandits 1860)

Consul Finn's House **1855**

Abraham's Vineyard Industrial Plantation founded, to provide work for poor Jews **1852**

Bishop Gobat's summer residence **1855**

JAFFA ROAD

Sultan grants St Anne's Church to Napoleon III of France **1856**

Sisters of Zion Orphanage and Convent **1857**

Status of the Holy Sepulchre and other Holy Places confirmed by the Sultan **1852**

Sidna Omar Mosque **1858**

'Deaconness House' German Protestant mission and pilgrims' hostel **1851**

Mamilla Pool

Mount Moriah

HARAM

Dome of the Rock repaired and strengthened by the Sultan **1853**

Bikur Cholim Hospital **1858**

Greek Orthodox Clerical Seminary established in the Monastery of the Cross **1852**

Montefiore Land Purchase **1855**

Consul Finn's Summer Villa **1853**

Beit Menachem Centre of Study (Habad brotherhood) **1858**

Misgav Ladach hospital **1854**

Bishop Gobat's School **1855**

Jewish Almhouses **1858**

Sultan's Pool

Mount Zion

Talbiye
British Consul Finn, organizes work for poor Jews **1853**

CAMEL TRACK TO GAZA

'Nothing equals the misery and the sufferings of the Jews at Jerusalem, inhabiting the most filthy quarter of the town, called hareth-el-yahoud, in the quarter of dirt, between the Zion and the Moriah, where their synagogues are situated – the constant object of Mussulman oppression and intolerance, insulted by the Greeks, persecuted by the Latins, and living only upon the scanty alms transmitted by their European brethren'.

KARL MARX
'NEW YORK DAILY TRIBUNE'
15 APRIL 1854

CRIMEAN WAR

'The Jewish alms from Russia failed. The Easter pilgrims did not arrive. There was such a lack of money, that even the Moslem population suffered hunger. The poor Jews starved.....A few kind Christian people, chiefly ladies, at Jerusalem, gave relief as they could, and wrote home for help.... The distribution immediately commenced, partly by means of an association of Christian ladies of various nations called the 'Sarah Society', who visit the poor Jewesses at their homes'.

'THE JERUSALEM MISCELLANY'
1855

'the sedentary population of Jerusalem numbers about 15,500 souls, of whom 4,000 are Mussulmans and 8,000 Jews. The Mussulmans forming about a fourth part of the whole, and consisting of Turks, Arabs, and Moors, are, of course, the masters in every respect'.

KARL MARX
'NEW YORK DAILY TRIBUNE'
15 APRIL 1854

Map 22

Plate 32 The Schneller Orphanage: a photograph taken in 1900, when it was being used as a Barracks by the Ottoman army.

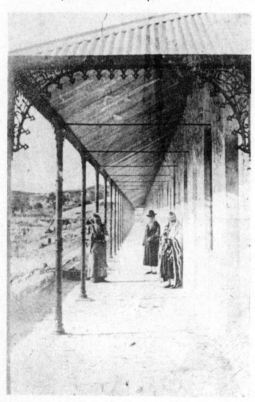

Plate 33 Three aged Jews in the porch of the "Montefiore Houses" a photograph taken in the 1860s. Montefiore chose as the mottoes for his seal of 1866 two biblical quotations: "The Holy City Jerusalem shall be built in our days, amen" and "Let the poor and needy praise thy name". During the fighting in 1948 the Montefiore houses were damaged, and, being just within the Israeli side of the subsequent Armistice line, they fell into serious disrepair. After 1967, when the city was re-united under a single administration, the Jerusalem Foundation restored the houses (see Map 59), turning them into guest houses for visiting artists, musicians and scholars from all over the world.

JERUSALEM IN THE 1860s

'No gas, no oil, no torch, no wax lights up the streets and archways of Jerusalem by night. Half an hour after gunfire the bazaar is cleared, the shops and baths are closed, the camels stalled, the narrow ways deserted'.
WILLIAM HEPWORTH DIXON 1866

' when a European is walking through Jerusalem by night, he is always followed by a number of canine attendants, and greeted at every step with growls and howls'.
ERMETE PIEROTTI
'CUSTOMS AND TRADITIONS OF PALESTINE' 1864

RUSSIAN HOSPICE

'This immense establishment is furnished with dormitories, refectories, chapel, reading-rooms, hospitals etc., and for cleanliness and good management would compare favourably with any institution of the kind in Europe'. BESANT & PALMER 'JERUSALEM' 1871

'The traveller will be vexed to see a mass of ugly buildings erected by the Russians, principally for the benefit of pilgrims'.
COOK'S HANDBOOK, 1876

THE OLD CITY

'Rags, wretchedness, poverty, and dirt, those signs and symbols that indicate the presence of Moslem rule more surely than the crescent-flag itself, abound. Lepers, cripples, the blind, and the idiotic assail you on every hand..... Jerusalem is mournful, and dreary, and lifeless. I would not desire to live here'.
MARK TWAIN
'THE INNOCENTS ABROAD' 1869

German Orphanage
† Founded by the Protestant missionary Ludwig Schneller
1860

CARRIAGE ROAD TO JAFFA COMPLETED 1868

Russian Compound:
Hospice for 1000 pilgrims
Purchase completed 1860
Buildings opened 1864

Talitha Kumi Girls School
founded by the Kaiserwerth Deaconesses from Rhineland-Westphalia
1865

Nahalat Shiva
JEWISH QUARTER 1869

Leper's hospital
1867

Mahane Israel
JEWISH QUARTER 1867

English Sanatorium
1864

Austrian Hospice
1863

Mount of Olives or 'Olivet'

Iron dome of the Church of the Holy Sepulchre: built with the Sultan's permission, at joint expense of France and Russia
1868

Roadway inside Jaffa Gate paved by the Turks
1864

Sultan's Pool

Mishkenot Sha'ananim
Montefiore Houses
1860

Evelina de Rothschild Girls School
1864

Hurva Synagogue
rebuilt and rededicated
1864

BETHLEHEM ROAD

'The Pasha has made his first attempt at road-making on this route. But, like all his other attempts in the direction of civilisation, it has been spasmodic, fitful, reluctant and has stopped short whenever his exchequer threatened to become a little shallow. You have, therefore, road-making in all its degrees on this first journey – some places finished, many more half-finished, and therefore intolerably rough and impassable, and others little more than marked off, and scarcely touched as yet by the spade or the mattock.'
ANDREW THOMSON 1869

☼ New Jewish buildings, 1860s.
† New Christian buildings, 1860s.

' while the Mohammedans are the masters, the Jews form the decided majority, being, it is likely, not far short of 8000. They come in a constant stream from every part of the world, many of them on pilgrimages, by which they hope to acquire a large fund of merit, and then return again to their native country; the greater number that they may die in the city of their fathers, and obtain the most cherished wish of their heart by being buried on Mount Olivet; and it is remarkable that they cling with a strange preference to that part of the city which is nearest the site of their ancient Temple, as if they still took pleasure in its stones, and its very dust were dear to them'.
ANDREW THOMSON 1869

| 0 | yards | 500 |
| 0 | metres | 500 |

POPULATION ESTIMATE OF 1868 IN 'THE JERUSALEM ALMANACK'

Jews	9,000
Muslims	5,000
Christians	4,000
TOTAL POPULATION	**18,000**

21 synagogues ⎫ listed in
11 mosques ⎬ the
21 convents ⎭ Almanack

Map 23

43

Plate 34   Robinson's arch, at the western wall of the Temple Mount. Behind it, the Moghrabi Quarter; to the left, Captain Warren's excavations. From a print from the *Survey of Western Palestine*, published in 1884.

Plate 35   Excavations at Wilson's Arch, underneath the Temple Mount. A print from the *Survey of Western Palestine*.

ARCHAEOLOGICAL EXPLORATIONS 1863-1914

◉ Some of the principal archaeological sites excavated between 1863 and 1914, with the date of excavation, and name of the archaeologist in charge.

In 1863 a French archaeologist, de Saulcy, began excavations at the Tomb of the Kings. In 1865 the Palestine Exploration Fund was set up in Britain; its first excavations in Jerusalem were undertaken by a British army officer, Captain Warren who, from 1867 to 1870 dug at fourteen different sites, seeking to uncover the city's biblical and Christian past. Following Warren, a succession of British, European and American archaeologists strove to reveal more and more of the City's history, making important progress by 1914.

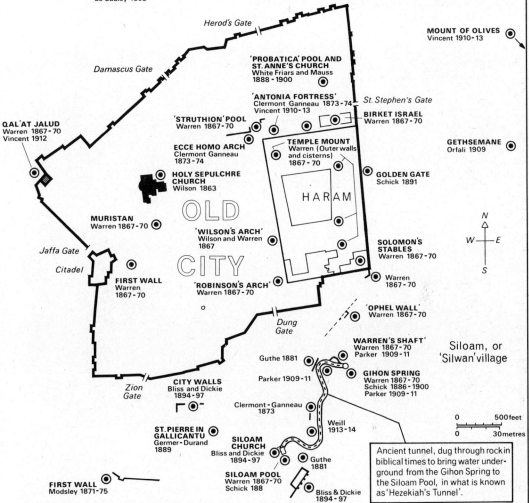

TOMB OF THE KINGS
de Saulcy 1863

Herod's Gate

MOUNT OF OLIVES
Vincent 1910-13

Damascus Gate

'PROBATICA' POOL AND ST. ANNE'S CHURCH
White Friars and Mauss 1888-1900

'ANTONIA FORTRESS'
Clermont Ganneau 1873-74
Vincent 1910-13

St. Stephen's Gate

'STRUTHION' POOL
Warren 1867-70

BIRKET ISRAEL
Warren 1867-70

QAL'AT JALUD
Warren 1867-70
Vincent 1912

ECCE HOMO ARCH
Clermont Ganneau 1873-74

TEMPLE MOUNT
Warren (Outer walls and cisterns) 1867-70

GETHSEMANE
Orfali 1909

HOLY SEPULCHRE CHURCH
Wilson 1863

HARAM

GOLDEN GATE
Schick 1891

MURISTAN
Warren 1867-70

OLD

'WILSON'S ARCH'
Wilson and Warren 1867

Jaffa Gate

Citadel

CITY

SOLOMON'S STABLES
Warren 1867-70

N
W — E
S

FIRST WALL
Warren 1867-70

'ROBINSON'S ARCH'
Warren 1867-70

Warren 1867-70

'OPHEL WALL'
Warren 1867-70

Dung Gate

'WARREN'S SHAFT'
Warren 1867-70
Parker 1909-11

Siloam, or 'Silwan' village

Zion Gate

CITY WALLS
Bliss and Dickie 1894-97

Guthe 1881

Parker 1909-11

GIHON SPRING
Warren 1867-70
Schick 1886-1900
Parker 1909-11

Clermont-Ganneau 1873

Weill 1913-14

0   500 feet
0   30 metres

ST. PIERRE IN GALLICANTU
Germer-Durand 1889

SILOAM CHURCH
Bliss and Dickie 1894-97

Guthe 1881

Ancient tunnel, dug through rock in biblical times to bring water underground from the Gihon Spring to the Siloam Pool, in what is known as 'Hezekiah's Tunnel'.

FIRST WALL
Modsley 1871-75

SILOAM POOL
Warren 1867-70
Schick 188

Bliss & Dickie 1894-97

'Showers of stones and streams of loose and treacherous shingle were common occurrences. In some places the earth was so poisoned by sewage, that the hands of the workmen broke out into festering sores; in other places the air was found to be so impure, that the candles refused to burn.... In another instance, the water from a periodic spring so increased upon them, that they were obliged to flee before it; and when it swelled up to Captain Warren's neck, he could only preserve the candle from extinction by carrying it in his mouth'.

ANDREW THOMSON 1869

'Our progress through these passages had been rapid, but unhappily the hammer-blows, resounding through the hollow walls in so unwonted a manner, alarmed the modern representative of the High Priest. Infuriate with anger, the fine old sheikh would listen to no reasoning: but repairing to the south-east angle of the old Temple enclosure, mounted its battlements and summoned the Sheikh of Siloam to stand forth and answer for his misdeeds. With full turban and long flowing robes, edges tipped with fur, the old man stood, on the edge of the steep masonry, stamping his feet with rage and bellowing imprecations'.

CHARLES WARREN 1874

Map 24

45

Plate 36 Seven "Ashkenazim", or "German Jews", as they were described in the caption to a photograph published in 1876 by the British explorer, Captain Charles Warren, in his book *Underground Jerusalem,* in which he wrote: "There is an irrepressible pride and presumption about this fragile wayward people of Ashkenaz that I could not help admiring; dressed in greasy rags, they stalk about the Holy City with as much dignity as though they were dressed in the richest garments, and give way to no one; years of oppression have in no way quelled their ancient spirit, and if they could only be induced to work and become united, they would be a very formidable race, for their courage and fortitude makes up for the want of stamina." Warren added: "They are among the most fanatical of mortals and can only believe in their own observances, and look with disgust upon the freedom from ceremony of even the strictest of Jews of our own country".

THE JEWISH QUARTER OF THE OLD CITY IN 1865

By 1864 the resident Jewish population of Jerusalem constituted a majority of the City's inhabitants, according to the British Consul in Jerusalem, Noel Temple Moore, who estimated the total population of the City at 15,000: 8,000 Jews, 4,500 Muslim Arabs, and 2,500 Christians and Christian Arabs. All 8,000 Jews lived within the Old City, mostly in the Jewish Quarter.

⌐ Southern wall of the Old City.

= Roads and alleyways.

▨ South west corner of the Haram, or Temple Mount.

✡ Sixteen synagogues in the Jewish Quarter identified by Dr. Sandreczki in his street-by-street survey of 1865.

▣ Other buildings identified by Sandreczki.

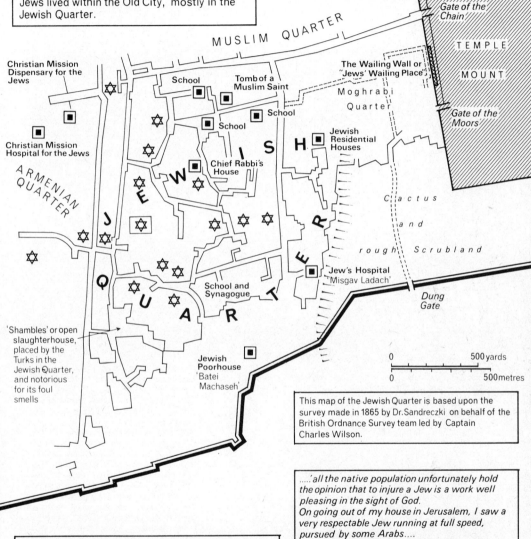

MUSLIM QUARTER

Christian Mission Dispensary for the Jews

Christian Mission Hospital for the Jews

ARMENIAN QUARTER

School

Tomb of a Muslim Saint

School

School

Chief Rabbi's House

J E W I S H   Q U A R T E R

The Wailing Wall or "Jews' Wailing Place"

Moghrabi Quarter

Jewish Residential Houses

TEMPLE MOUNT

Gate of the Chain

Gate of the Moors

Cactus and rough Scrubland

Jew's Hospital 'Misgav Ladach'

Dung Gate

School and Synagogue

'Shambles' or open slaughterhouse, placed by the Turks in the Jewish Quarter, and notorious for its foul smells

Jewish Poorhouse 'Batei Machaseh'

0   500 yards
0   500 metres

This map of the Jewish Quarter is based upon the survey made in 1865 by Dr. Sandreczki on behalf of the British Ordnance Survey team led by Captain Charles Wilson.

'The Jerusalem synagogues, however, are not adorned like many of those in our European capitals, such as we have seen at Leghorn and Frankfurt, probably in order to avoid tempting the cupidity of unscrupulous Moslem rulers. It is indeed remarkable in how many ways the Jews keep hold of their country as with a trembling hand, and are reluctant to let go the traces and the records of a glorious past'.
ANDREW THOMSON
'IN THE HOLY LAND' 1869

.....'all the native population unfortunately hold the opinion that to injure a Jew is a work well pleasing in the sight of God.
On going out of my house in Jerusalem, I saw a very respectable Jew running at full speed, pursued by some Arabs....
The Jews in the East, as I have had proof over and over again, seek not to destroy the life of others but to preserve their own, enduring with meekness, constancy and patience, the insults and injuries which they receive from Christians and Mohammedans alike'.
ERMETE PIEROTTI
'CUSTOMS AND TRADITIONS OF PALESTINE' 1864

© Martin Gilbert 1977

Map 25

47

Plate 37   The road from Jaffa to Jerusalem. A photograph, taken by the American photographer Robert Bain in 1894, of the horse-drawn carriage of Howard's Hotel.

Plate 38   Russian pilgrims waiting at Jerusalem Railway Station; a photograph taken in about 1900. Stephen Graham, an Englishman who accompanied a group of Russian pilgrims in 1912, wrote in the following year: "It was amazing to me to see the extent to which the pilgrims sought in Jerusalem tokens for the clothing of their dead bodies, and how much their thoughts were centred on death and the final resurrection morning. They sanctified crosses at the grave, little ones to wear round their necks in the tomb, and larger ones to lie on their breasts; they brought their death-shrouds and cross-embroidered caps to dip them in Jordan; they took Jerusalem earth to put in their coffins, and even had their arms tattooed with the word Jerusalem, and with pictures of the Virgin; so that they might lie so marked in the grave, and indeed that they might rise again so marked, and show it in heaven. By these things they felt they obtained a sort of sanctity".

ROAD AND RAIL LINKS TO THE COAST AFTER 1868

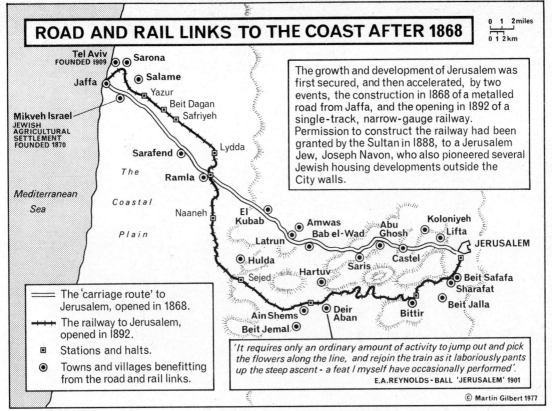

0 1 2miles
0 1 2km

The growth and development of Jerusalem was first secured, and then accelerated, by two events, the construction in 1868 of a metalled road from Jaffa, and the opening in 1892 of a single-track, narrow-gauge railway. Permission to construct the railway had been granted by the Sultan in 1888, to a Jerusalem Jew, Joseph Navon, who also pioneered several Jewish housing developments outside the City walls.

Tel Aviv FOUNDED 1909
Sarona
Salame
Jaffa
Yazur
Beit Dagan
Safriyeh
Mikveh Israel JEWISH AGRICULTURAL SETTLEMENT FOUNDED 1870
Lydda
Sarafend
The Coastal Plain
Ramla
Mediterranean Sea
Naaneh
El Kubab
Amwas
Bab el-Wad
Abu Ghosh
Koloniyeh
Lifta
Latrun
Castel
JERUSALEM
Hulda
Sejed
Hartuv
Saris
Beit Safafa
Sharafat
Ain Shems
Deir Aban
Bittir
Beit Jalla
Beit Jemal

— The 'carriage route' to Jerusalem, opened in 1868.

+++ The railway to Jerusalem, opened in 1892.

▫ Stations and halts.

◉ Towns and villages benefitting from the road and rail links.

'It requires only an ordinary amount of activity to jump out and pick the flowers along the line, and rejoin the train as it laboriously pants up the steep ascent - a feat I myself have occasionally performed'.

E.A.REYNOLDS-BALL 'JERUSALEM' 1901

© Martin Gilbert 1977

CHRISTIAN PILGRIMAGES AROUND JERUSALEM

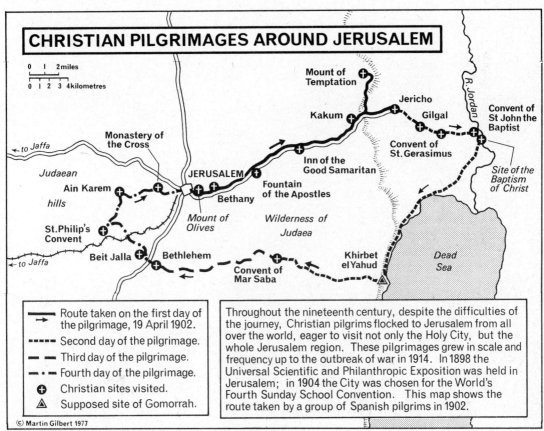

0 1 2miles
0 1 2 3 4kilometres

to Jaffa
Judaean hills
Ain Karem
St.Philip's Convent
Monastery of the Cross
JERUSALEM
Bethany
Mount of Olives
Fountain of the Apostles
Beit Jalla
Bethlehem
to Jaffa
Convent of Mar Saba
Wilderness of Judaea
Mount of Temptation
Kakum
Inn of the Good Samaritan
Convent of St. Gerasimus
Jericho
Gilgal
Convent of St John the Baptist
Site of the Baptism of Christ
Khirbet el Yahud
Dead Sea
R. Jordan

— Route taken on the first day of the pilgrimage, 19 April 1902.

----- Second day of the pilgrimage.

– – Third day of the pilgrimage.

–·– Fourth day of the pilgrimage.

✛ Christian sites visited.

▲ Supposed site of Gomorrah.

© Martin Gilbert 1977

Throughout the nineteenth century, despite the difficulties of the journey, Christian pilgrims flocked to Jerusalem from all over the world, eager to visit not only the Holy City, but the whole Jerusalem region. These pilgrimages grew in scale and frequency up to the outbreak of war in 1914. In 1898 the Universal Scientific and Philanthropic Exposition was held in Jerusalem; in 1904 the City was chosen for the World's Fourth Sunday School Convention. This map shows the route taken by a group of Spanish pilgrims in 1902.

Map 27

Plate 39   A Shoemaker's Shop, Jerusalem. "Jewish shoemakers at work." An engraving by W.J. Palmer, published in 1878 in Colonel Wilson's *Picturesque Palestine*.

Plate 40   A Street Cafe, Jerusalem. "A Bedouin and peasant playing at a game called dameh". An engraving by Harley, published in *Picturesque Palestine* in 1878.

JERUSALEM IN THE 1870s

1870 The first Georgian Jews arrive from the Caucasus (**200** had come by 1875).

1876 Cook's Tourists' Handbook estimates Jerusalem's population at **8,000** to **9,000** Jews out of a total population of between **16,000** and **20,000**.

1877 The Jerusalem newspaper 'Judaea and Jerusalem' advocates Jewish agricultural settlements in Palestine.

1878 Jews from Jerusalem help to establish an agricultural settlement on the coastal plain, at Petah Tikvah.

AL AKSA MOSQUE

'The Muslim guide will wax eloquent upon this, his favourite subject, the connection between the day of judgement and the Masjid el Aksa. (After the Anti-Christ has been killed) the victors will then proceed to a general massacre of the Jews in and around the Holy City, and every tree and every stone shall cry out and say: "I have a Jew beneath me, slay him". Having done this, the Messiah will break the crosses and kill the pigs (Christians), after which the Millenium will set in'.

BESANT & PALMER
'JERUSALEM' 1871

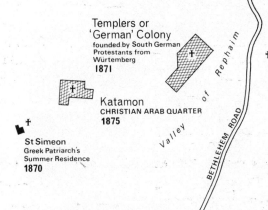

NABLUS ROAD

Tomb of Simon the Just
✡ Site bought by Jewish worshippers
1876

Batei Yaakov
JEWISH QUARTER
1877

Tomb of the Kings
Site bought by a Jewish family from France
1878

Bab-al Zahra
CHRISTIAN ARAB QUARTER
1875

Batei David
JEWISH QUARTER
1877

Mea Shearim
JEWISH QUARTER
1874

Batei Nissan Bek
JEWISH QUARTER
1879

Karm el-Sheikh
MUSLIM ARAB QUARTER
1870s

JAFFA ROAD

Mishkenot Yisrael
JEWISH QUARTER
1875

Musrara
MUSLIM ARAB QUARTER
1875

Herod's Gate

Mount of Olives

Even Yisrael
JEWISH QUARTER
1875

VIA DOLOROSA

Ratisbonne Monastery
Founded by French-Jewish converts to Christianity
1874

Mamilla Pool

Jaffa Gate

Moghrabi Mosque
1871

Dome of the Rock

Pater Noster
French Carmelite Sisters, Church and Convent
1873

Collège des Frères
Franciscan Boys School
1876

Al Aksa Mosque

Greek Orthodox Hospital
1876

Sultan's Pool

Mount Zion

Sultan Abdul Aziz fits stained glass windows in Al Aksa, and repairs ceiling, walls and floors of Dome of the Rock, 1874. Sultan Abdul Hamid II provides carpets and tiles, 1876

Templers or 'German' Colony
founded by South German Protestants from Würtemberg
1871

Valley of Rephaim

Nissim Bak Synagogue 'Tiferet Yisrael'
1874

Abu Tor
MIXED MUSLIM & CHRISTIAN ARAB QUARTER
1870s

Katamon
CHRISTIAN ARAB QUARTER
1875

BETHLEHEM ROAD

St Simeon
Greek Patriarch's Summer Residence
1870

```
0    yards    500
0    metres   500
```

✡ New Jewish buildings, 1870s.

✝ New Christian and Christian Arab buildings.

☾ New Muslim buildings, repairs and renovations.

VIA DOLOROSA

'No one can traverse its curious zig-zags and look at its "holy places" with indifference, as it is sacred with the tears of many generations of pilgrims, who, according to their faith, strove to follow in the footsteps of the Lord. As a mere hard and dry matter of fact, however, there is no historical evidence whatever for the street was not even known until the four-teenth century'.

COOK'S HANDBOOK
1876

© Martin Gilbert 1977

Map 28

51

Plate 41   The British Ophthalmic Hospital, founded in 1882, on the road to Bethlehem, by the Order of St. John. It was partly blown up by the Turks in 1917 and again badly damaged in 1948, during the first Arab-Israeli war. This photograph was taken in about 1900.

Plate 42   The German Catholic Hospice, later Schmidt College, founded in 1886, outside the Damascus Gate. During the British Mandate it served first as the 'Governorate', and later as the Royal Air Force headquarters. From another photograph taken in about 1900.

JERUSALEM IN THE 1880s

POPULATION IN 1889	
Jews	25,000
Christians	7,175
Muslims	7,000
TOTAL POPULATION	**39,175**

CHRISTIAN SECTS	
Greek Orthodox	4,000
Catholics (Latins)	2,000
Armenians	500
Protestants	300
Greek Catholics	150
Copts	100
Abyssinians	75
Armenian Catholics	50

✡ Principal new Jewish houses built in the **1880s**.

✝ Principal new Christian houses built in the **1880s**.

⚲ Principal new Muslim houses built in the **1880s**.

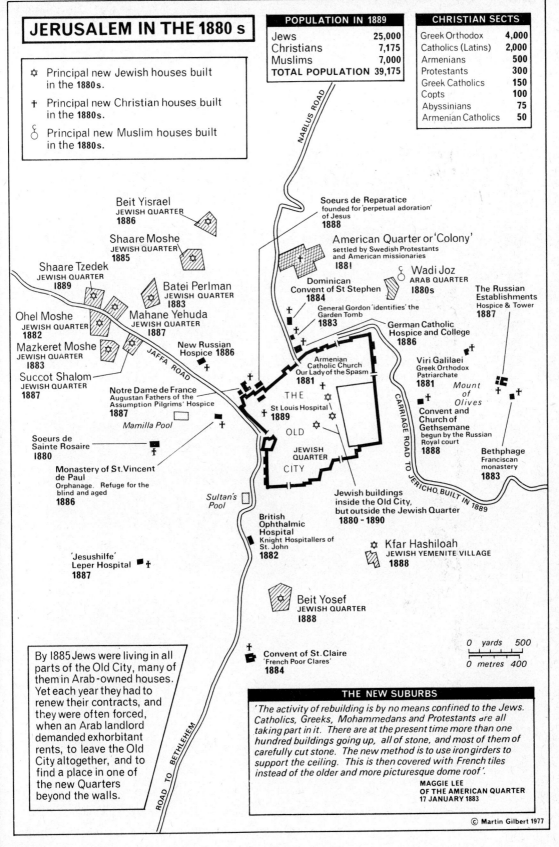

NABLUS ROAD

Beit Yisrael
JEWISH QUARTER
1886

Shaare Moshe
JEWISH QUARTER
1885

Shaare Tzedek
JEWISH QUARTER
1889

Batei Perlman
JEWISH QUARTER
1883

Ohel Moshe
JEWISH QUARTER
1882

Mahane Yehuda
JEWISH QUARTER
1887

Mazkeret Moshe
JEWISH QUARTER
1883

Succot Shalom
JEWISH QUARTER
1887

JAFFA ROAD

Notre Dame de France
Augustan Fathers of the
Assumption Pilgrims' Hospice
1887

Mamilla Pool

**Soeurs de
Sainte Rosaire
1880**

**New Russian
Hospice 1886**

Soeurs de Reparatice
founded for 'perpetual adoration'
of Jesus
1888

American Quarter or 'Colony'
settled by Swedish Protestants
and American missionaries
1881

**Dominican
Convent of St Stephen**
1884

**General Gordon 'identifies' the
Garden Tomb**
1883

Wadi Joz
ARAB QUARTER
1880s

**The Russian
Establishments**
Hospice & Tower
1887

**German Catholic
Hospice and College**
1886

**Armenian
Catholic Church
Our Lady of the Spasm
1881**

THE

**St Louis Hospital
1889**

OLD

JEWISH
QUARTER

CITY

Viri Galilaei
Greek Orthodox
Patriarchate
1881

*Mount
of
Olives*

**Convent and
Church of
Gethsemane**
begun by the Russian
Royal court
1888

Bethphage
Franciscan
monastery
1883

CARRIAGE ROAD TO JERICHO, BUILT IN 1889

**Jewish buildings
inside the Old City,
but outside the Jewish Quarter
1880 - 1890**

**Monastery of St. Vincent
de Paul**
Orphanage. Refuge for the
blind and aged
1886

*Sultan's
Pool*

**British
Ophthalmic
Hospital**
Knight Hospitallers of
St. John
1882

Kfar Hashiloah
JEWISH YEMENITE VILLAGE
1888

**'Jesushilfe'
Leper Hospital
1887**

Beit Yosef
JEWISH QUARTER
1888

0	yards	500
0	metres	400

Convent of St. Claire
'French Poor Clares'
1884

ROAD TO BETHLEHEM

By 1885 Jews were living in all parts of the Old City, many of them in Arab-owned houses. Yet each year they had to renew their contracts, and they were often forced, when an Arab landlord demanded exhorbitant rents, to leave the Old City altogether, and to find a place in one of the new Quarters beyond the walls.

THE NEW SUBURBS

'The activity of rebuilding is by no means confined to the Jews. Catholics, Greeks, Mohammedans and Protestants are all taking part in it. There are at the present time more than one hundred buildings going up, all of stone, and most of them of carefully cut stone. The new method is to use iron girders to support the ceiling. This is then covered with French tiles instead of the older and more picturesque dome roof'.

**MAGGIE LEE
OF THE AMERICAN QUARTER
17 JANUARY 1883**

© Martin Gilbert 1977

Map 29

53

Plate 43   Outside the Jaffa Gate. "The road from Jerusalem to Bethlehem", a photograph taken by Robert Bain in 1894.

Plate 44   The Installation of the Chief Rabbi of Jerusalem in 1893, at the Ben Zakkai synagogue in the Jewish Quarter of the Old City. The Chief Rabbi was elected by the Council of Sages of the Jewish community, and had been given by the Ottoman Empire, from 1840, the official title of "Hacham Bashi", whose community judgments were recognised by the Turkish authorities.

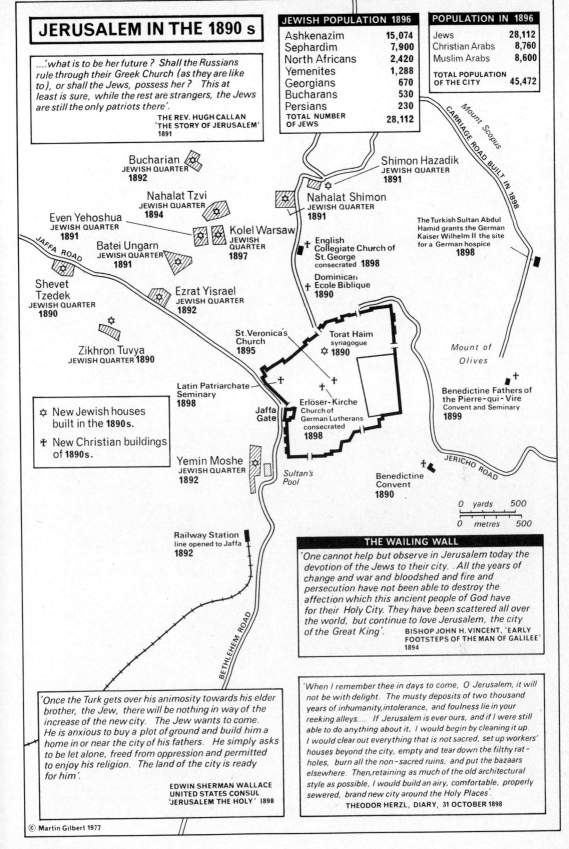

JERUSALEM IN THE 1890s

...'what is to be her future? Shall the Russians rule through their Greek Church (as they are like to), or shall the Jews, possess her? This at least is sure, while the rest are strangers, the Jews are still the only patriots there'.
THE REV. HUGH CALLAN 'THE STORY OF JERUSALEM' 1891

JEWISH POPULATION 1896

Ashkenazim	15,074
Sephardim	7,900
North Africans	2,420
Yemenites	1,288
Georgians	670
Bucharans	530
Persians	230
TOTAL NUMBER OF JEWS	28,112

POPULATION IN 1896

Jews	28,112
Christian Arabs	8,760
Muslim Arabs	8,600
TOTAL POPULATION OF THE CITY	45,472

CARRIAGE ROAD BUILT IN 1898

Mount Scopus

Bucharian
JEWISH QUARTER
1892

Shimon Hazadik
JEWISH QUARTER
1891

Nahalat Tzvi
JEWISH QUARTER
1894

Nahalat Shimon
JEWISH QUARTER
1891

Even Yehoshua
JEWISH QUARTER
1891

Kolel Warsaw
JEWISH QUARTER
1897

The Turkish Sultan Abdul Hamid grants the German Kaiser Wilhelm II the site for a German hospice
1898

Batei Ungarn
JEWISH QUARTER
1891

JAFFA ROAD

English Collegiate Church of St. George
consecrated 1898

Shevet Tzedek
JEWISH QUARTER
1890

Ezrat Yisrael
JEWISH QUARTER
1892

Dominican Ecole Biblique
1890

Zikhron Tuvya
JEWISH QUARTER 1890

Mount of Olives

St.Veronica's Church
1895

Torat Haim
synagogue
1890

New Jewish houses built in the 1890s.

New Christian buildings of 1890s.

Latin Patriarchate Seminary
1898

Benedictine Fathers of the Pierre-qui-Vire Convent and Seminary
1899

Jaffa Gate

Erlöser-Kirche
Church of German Lutherans
consecrated 1898

JERICHO ROAD

Yemin Moshe
JEWISH QUARTER
1892

Sultan's Pool

Benedictine Convent
1890

0	yards	500
0	metres	500

Railway Station
line opened to Jaffa
1892

BETHLEHEM ROAD

THE WAILING WALL

'One cannot help but observe in Jerusalem today the devotion of the Jews to their city. All the years of change and war and bloodshed and fire and persecution have not been able to destroy the affection which this ancient people of God have for their Holy City. They have been scattered all over the world, but continue to love Jerusalem, the city of the Great King'.
BISHOP JOHN H. VINCENT, 'EARLY FOOTSTEPS OF THE MAN OF GALILEE' 1894

'Once the Turk gets over his animosity towards his elder brother, the Jew, there will be nothing in way of the increase of the new city. The Jew wants to come. He is anxious to buy a plot of ground and build him a home in or near the city of his fathers. He simply asks to be let alone, freed from oppression and permitted to enjoy his religion. The land of the city is ready for him'.
EDWIN SHERMAN WALLACE
UNITED STATES CONSUL
'JERUSALEM THE HOLY' 1898

'When I remember thee in days to come, O Jerusalem, it will not be with delight. The musty deposits of two thousand years of inhumanity, intolerance, and foulness lie in your reeking alleys.... If Jerusalem is ever ours, and if I were still able to do anything about it, I would begin by cleaning it up. I would clear out everything that is not sacred, set up workers' houses beyond the city, empty and tear down the filthy rat-holes, burn all the non-sacred ruins, and put the bazaars elsewhere. Then, retaining as much of the old architectural style as possible, I would build an airy, comfortable, properly sewered, brand new city around the Holy Places'.
THEODOR HERZL, DIARY, 31 OCTOBER 1898

© Martin Gilbert 1977

Map 30

Plate 45   Franciscan monks; a photograph taken for the American Colony, and forming number 580 of its pre-1914 photograph collection, which was sold to tourists and pilgrims visiting Jerusalem.

Plate 46   Students of the Bezalel Art School learning Hebrew, at the turn of the century. The school had been founded in Jerusalem in 1906 by Boris Schatz, court sculptor of King Ferdinand of Bulgaria. Schatz settled in Jerusalem, dying there in 1932.

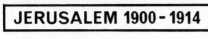

JERUSALEM 1900-1914

POPULATION: OTTOMAN SUBJECTS 1905	
Jews	**40,000**
Christian Arabs	**10,900**
Muslim Arabs	**8,000**
TOTAL POPULATION	**58,900**
By 1914 the Jewish population was **45,000**	

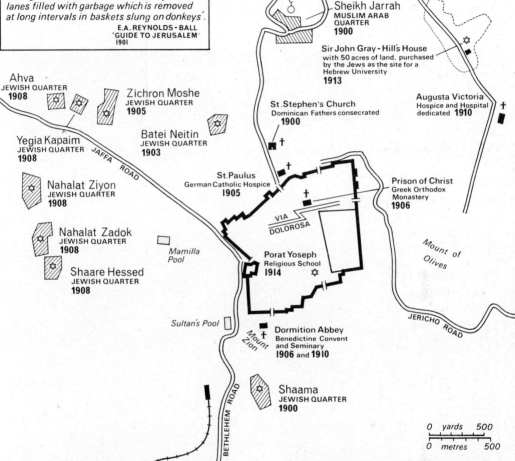

NABLUS ROAD

Mount Scopus

Sheikh Jarrah
MUSLIM ARAB
QUARTER
1900

Sir John Gray - Hill's House
with 50 acres of land, purchased by the Jews as the site for a Hebrew University
1913

Augusta Victoria
Hospice and Hospital
dedicated 1910

Ahva
JEWISH QUARTER
1908

Zichron Moshe
JEWISH QUARTER
1905

St. Stephen's Church
Dominican Fathers consecrated
1900

Yegia Kapaim
JEWISH QUARTER
1908

JAFFA ROAD

Batei Neitin
JEWISH QUARTER
1903

St. Paulus
German Catholic Hospice
1905

Prison of Christ
Greek Orthodox
Monastery
1906

Nahalat Ziyon
JEWISH QUARTER
1908

VIA DOLOROSA

Nahalat Zadok
JEWISH QUARTER
1908

Mamilla
Pool

Porat Yoseph
Religious School
1914

Mount of Olives

Shaare Hessed
JEWISH QUARTER
1908

JERICHO ROAD

Sultan's Pool

Mount Zion

Dormition Abbey
Benedictine Convent
and Seminary
1906 and 1910

BETHLEHEM ROAD

Shaama
JEWISH QUARTER
1900

| 0 | yards | 500 |
| 0 | metres | 500 |

© Martin Gilbert 1977

Map 31

57

Plate 47   A Jewish Suburb on the outskirts of Jerusalem before 1914.

Plate 48   The Austrian Post Office, inside the Jaffa Gate; a photograph taken in 1898. The Austrian Post began operation in 1859, followed by the Turkish in 1867, the French and German in 1900, the Russian in 1901 and the Italian in 1908. Within the Old City there were two Turkish branch offices, 'Quartier Israelite' in the Jewish Quarter from 1896, and 'Souk-el-Attarin' in the Muslim Quarter from 1907. There were also Turkish branch offices at the Railway Station from 1901, and at the Jewish suburbs of Mea Shearim from 1904, and Mahane Yehuda, from 1909.

THE GROWTH OF JERUSALEM BY 1914

By the time of the outbreak of war between Britain and Turkey, in 1914, there were nearly twice as many citizens of Jerusalem living outside the Old City as within it. The City's main thoroughfare had become the Jaffa Road, along which not only Jewish houses, but also foreign consulates, European Post Offices, hotels, shops and workshops were clustered. Both Jews and Arabs were attracted by the city's increasing prosperity and modernity. Between 1889 and 1912 the population of Jerusalem had nearly doubled, from 45,000 to 70,000; an increase, mostly by immigration, from outside Palestine, of both Jews and Arabs (some 20,000 more Jews and 11,000 more Arabs in 23 years)

- Jewish suburbs by 1914.
- Christian Arab suburbs by 1914.
- Muslim Arab suburbs by 1914.
- Areas of mixed Arab-Jewish, and European houses, shops and offices.

to Nablus

Mount Scopus

SHEIKH JARRAH

MEA SHEARIM

Jaffa Road

MUSLIM QUARTER

Damascus Gate

CHRISTIAN QUARTER

HARAM

THE OLD CITY

Jaffa Gate

JEWISH QUARTER

Mount of Olives or 'Olivet'

to Jericho

ARMENIAN QUARTER

YEMIN MOSHE

Mount Zion

SHAAMA

SILWAN

Greek Monastery of the Cross

to Gaza

KEFAR HASHILOAH

ABU TOR

0   600 yards

0   400 metres

'GERMAN' or WURTEMBURG COLONY

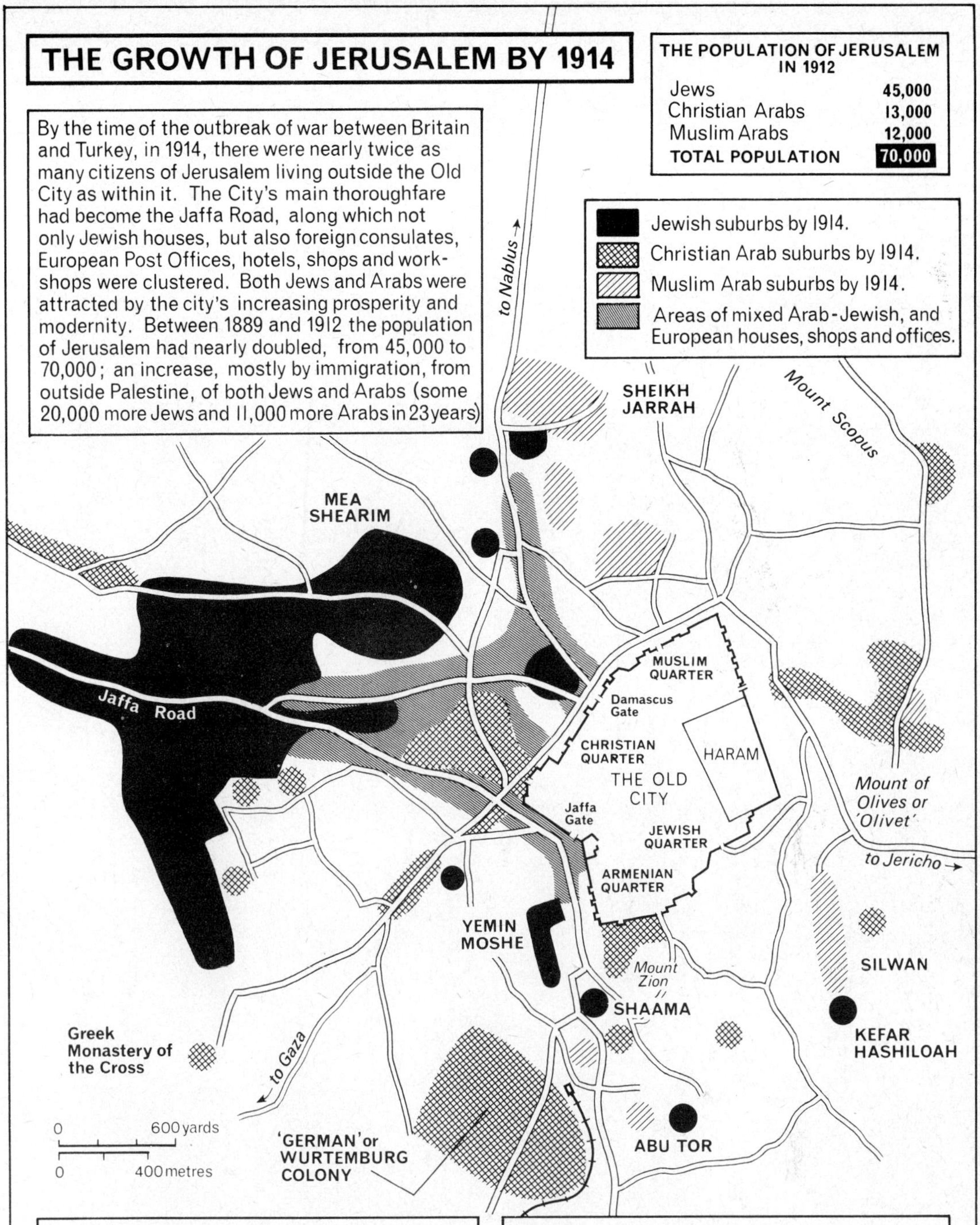

'Near the Jaffa Gate, inside the city, is the Grand New Hotel, kept by Marcos, a Catholic. A little further on, we came to the Central Hotel, kept by Amdurski, a Jew. Outside the city, on the Jaffa road, we come successively to the Park Hotel, kept by Hall; then farther on, to the left, the Hotel Hughes, kept by Hughes, an Englishman; and on the right, near the French Consulate, the little Hotel de France, kept by Dominique Bourrel'.

FATHER BARNABAS MEISTERMANN
'NEW GUIDE TO THE HOLY LAND'
1907

'If numerical superiority be a criterion of possession, and achievement a measure of power; if the higher civilisation be that of the more effective philanthropy, and true part and lot in the soil be that of him who restores it to cultivation; then, mysterious as may seem to us the workings of God's providence, the deep tragedy of their existence, the dark problem of their destiny, is approaching solution, and Jerusalem is for the Jews'.

MISS FREER
'INNER JERUSALEM'
1907

Map 32

59

Plate 49   Jewish soldiers of the Austro-Hungarian Army praying at the Wailing Wall while stationed in Jerusalem during the First World War.

Plate 50   Arabs, accused by the Turks of pro-British sympathies, and hanged outside the Jaffa Gate during the First World War. Among those hanged were two members of the Husseini family, the Mufti of Gaza and his son.

JERUSALEM AND THE FIRST WORLD WAR 1914 - 1917

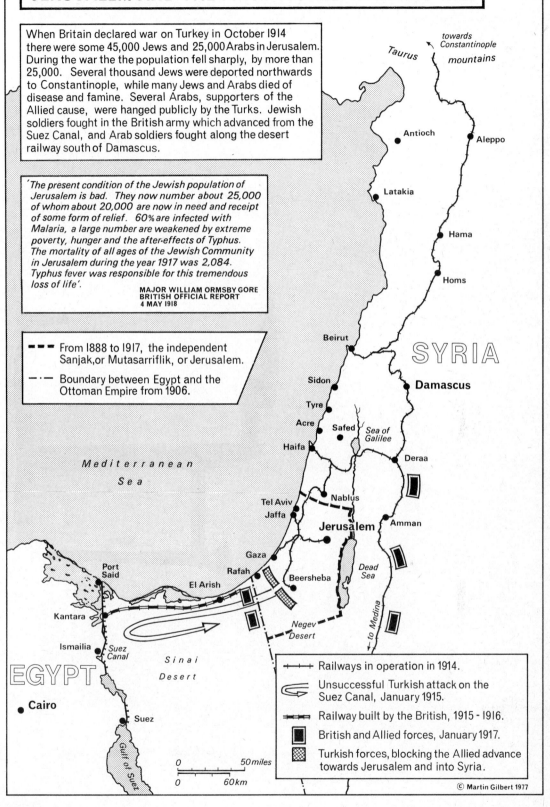

When Britain declared war on Turkey in October 1914 there were some 45,000 Jews and 25,000 Arabs in Jerusalem. During the war the the population fell sharply, by more than 25,000. Several thousand Jews were deported northwards to Constantinople, while many Jews and Arabs died of disease and famine. Several Arabs, supporters of the Allied cause, were hanged publicly by the Turks. Jewish soldiers fought in the British army which advanced from the Suez Canal, and Arab soldiers fought along the desert railway south of Damascus.

'The present condition of the Jewish population of Jerusalem is bad. They now number about 25,000 of whom about 20,000 are now in need and receipt of some form of relief. 60% are infected with Malaria, a large number are weakened by extreme poverty, hunger and the after-effects of Typhus. The mortality of all ages of the Jewish Community in Jerusalem during the year 1917 was 2,084. Typhus fever was responsible for this tremendous loss of life'.

MAJOR WILLIAM ORMSBY GORE
BRITISH OFFICIAL REPORT
4 MAY 1918

- - - From 1888 to 1917, the independent Sanjak, or Mutasarriflik, or Jerusalem.

- · - Boundary between Egypt and the Ottoman Empire from 1906.

towards Constantinople

Taurus mountains

Antioch
Aleppo
Latakia
Hama
Homs
Beirut
SYRIA
Sidon
Damascus
Tyre
Acre
Safed
Sea of Galilee
Haifa
Deraa
Mediterranean Sea
Tel Aviv
Nablus
Jaffa
Jerusalem
Amman
Gaza
Port Said
Rafah
Dead Sea
El Arish
Beersheba
Kantara
Negev Desert
Ismailia
Suez Canal
to Medina
EGYPT
Sinai Desert
Cairo
Suez
Gulf of Suez

+++ Railways in operation in 1914.

⟲ Unsuccessful Turkish attack on the Suez Canal, January 1915.

+++ Railway built by the British, 1915 - 1916.

■ British and Allied forces, January 1917.

▨ Turkish forces, blocking the Allied advance towards Jerusalem and into Syria.

0   50 miles
0   60 km

© Martin Gilbert 1977

Map 33

61

Plate 51 The surrender of Jerusalem on 9 December 1917. The Mayor (with walking stick) and the Chief of Police (far right) bring the flag of truce to Sergeants Hurcomb and Sedgewick of the 2/19th Battalion, London Regiment. Two days later, on 11 December, General Allenby made his official entry into the City, together with representatives of the French and Italian contingents which had fought on the Jerusalem front.

Plate 52 British soldiers and their armoured car at the Jaffa Gate, shortly after the British occupation of the city. During the battle for Jerusalem more than 3,600 British and 19,000 Turkish soldiers had been killed in action.

THE BRITISH CONQUEST OF JERUSALEM, DECEMBER 1917

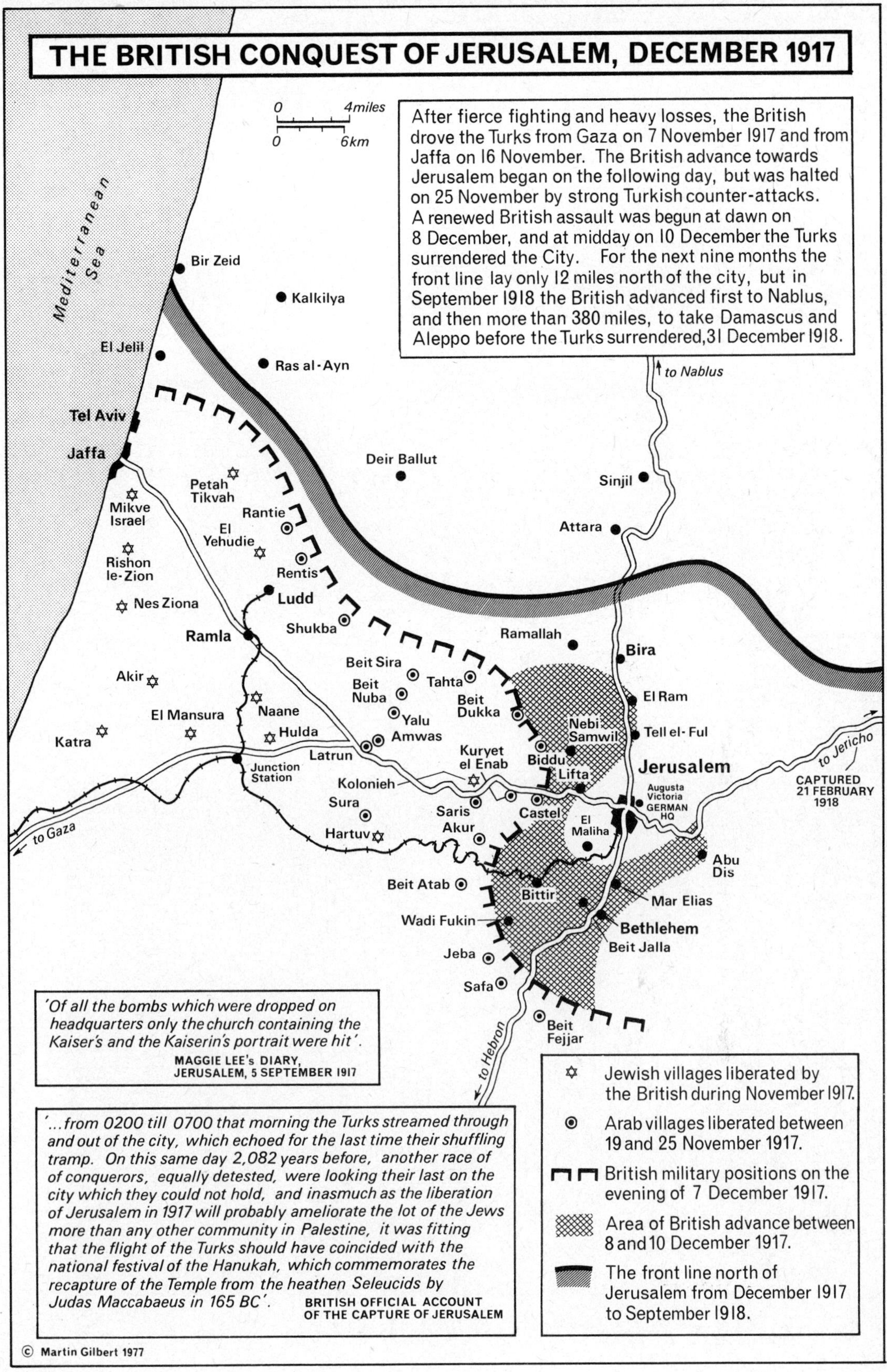

0   4 miles
0   6 km

After fierce fighting and heavy losses, the British drove the Turks from Gaza on 7 November 1917 and from Jaffa on 16 November. The British advance towards Jerusalem began on the following day, but was halted on 25 November by strong Turkish counter-attacks. A renewed British assault was begun at dawn on 8 December, and at midday on 10 December the Turks surrendered the City. For the next nine months the front line lay only 12 miles north of the city, but in September 1918 the British advanced first to Nablus, and then more than 380 miles, to take Damascus and Aleppo before the Turks surrendered, 31 December 1918.

Mediterranean Sea

to Nablus

Bir Zeid

Kalkilya

El Jelil

Ras al-Ayn

Tel Aviv

Jaffa

Deir Ballut

Sinjil

Petah Tikvah

Attara

Mikve Israel

Rantie

El Yehudie

Rishon le-Zion

Rentis

Nes Ziona

Ludd

Shukba

Ramallah

Bira

Ramla

Beit Sira

Tahta

El Ram

Akir

Beit Nuba

Beit Dukka

Naane

Yalu

Nebi Samwil

Tell el-Ful

El Mansura

Hulda

Amwas

Jerusalem

to Jericho

Katra

Latrun

Kuryet el Enab

Biddu

Junction Station

Kolonieh

Saris

Castel

Lifta

Augusta Victoria GERMAN HQ

CAPTURED 21 FEBRUARY 1918

Sura

Akur

El Maliha

Hartuv

Abu Dis

Beit Atab

Bittir

Mar Elias

to Gaza

Wadi Fukin

Bethlehem

Beit Jalla

Jeba

Safa

Beit Fejjar

to Hebron

'Of all the bombs which were dropped on headquarters only the church containing the Kaiser's and the Kaiserin's portrait were hit'.
MAGGIE LEE'S DIARY, JERUSALEM, 5 SEPTEMBER 1917

'...from 0200 till 0700 that morning the Turks streamed through and out of the city, which echoed for the last time their shuffling tramp. On this same day 2,082 years before, another race of conquerors, equally detested, were looking their last on the city which they could not hold, and inasmuch as the liberation of Jerusalem in 1917 will probably ameliorate the lot of the Jews more than any other community in Palestine, it was fitting that the flight of the Turks should have coincided with the national festival of the Hanukah, which commemorates the recapture of the Temple from the heathen Seleucids by Judas Maccabaeus in 165 BC'. BRITISH OFFICIAL ACCOUNT OF THE CAPTURE OF JERUSALEM

✡ Jewish villages liberated by the British during November 1917.

◉ Arab villages liberated between 19 and 25 November 1917.

⌐⌐ British military positions on the evening of 7 December 1917.

▨ Area of British advance between 8 and 10 December 1917.

▧ The front line north of Jerusalem from December 1917 to September 1918.

© Martin Gilbert 1977

Map 34

Plate 53   1918: British and Indian (Muslim) soldiers on guard in the Old City. A cordon of Indian Muslim officers and men was also established around the Haram enclosure, but, as a "political courtesy", the local Muslim doorkeepers were allowed to remain at their posts.

Plate 54   1918: Jewish soldiers of the British Army celebrate their first Passover in Jerusalem.

JERUSALEM UNDER BRITISH MILITARY RULE 1917 - 1920

In April 1918 the British Military Governor of Jerusalem, Sir Ronald Storrs, issued two edicts, one forbidding the demolition of ancient or historic buildings, the other forbidding the use of either stucco or corrugated iron within the city walls, "thus respecting", as Storrs explained on 15 March 1921, "the tradition of stone vaulting, the heritage in Jerusalem of an immemorial and a hallowed past".

Following the British occupation of Jerusalem, the British military authorities repaired and widened the railway line to the coast, built a narrow gauge railway to take military supplies to the front line, and repaired the much neglected city gates and walls.

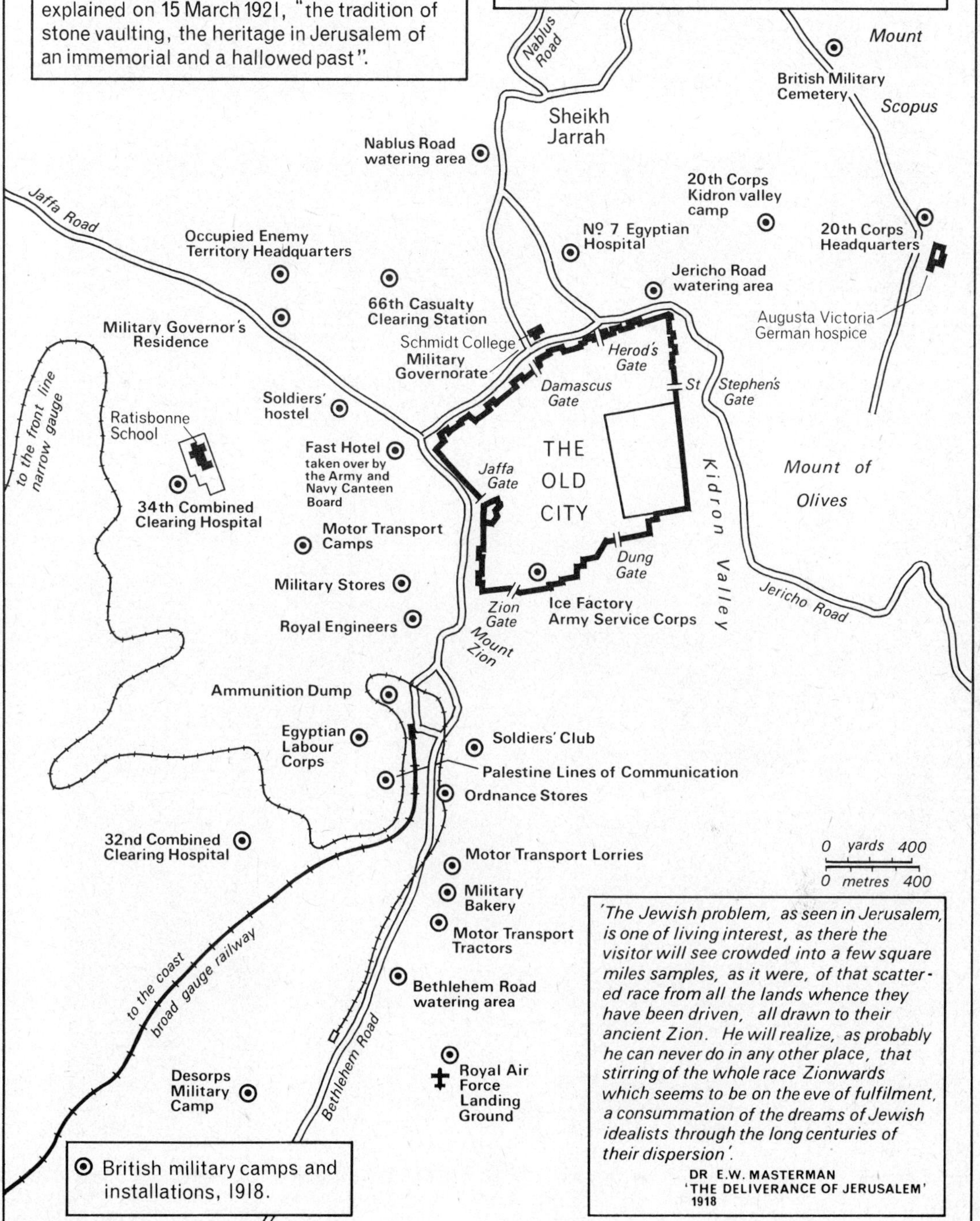

Nablus Road

Mount

British Military Cemetery

Scopus

Sheikh Jarrah

Nablus Road watering area

20th Corps Kidron valley camp

20th Corps Headquarters

Jaffa Road

Occupied Enemy Territory Headquarters

Nº 7 Egyptian Hospital

Jericho Road watering area

Military Governor's Residence

66th Casualty Clearing Station

Schmidt College Military Governorate

Augusta Victoria German hospice

Herod's Gate

Ratisbonne School

Soldiers' hostel

Damascus Gate

St Stephen's Gate

34th Combined Clearing Hospital

Fast Hotel taken over by the Army and Navy Canteen Board

THE OLD CITY

Jaffa Gate

Mount of Olives

Kidron Valley

to the front line narrow gauge

Motor Transport Camps

Military Stores

Royal Engineers

Zion Gate

Mount Zion

Dung Gate

Ice Factory Army Service Corps

Jericho Road

Ammunition Dump

Egyptian Labour Corps

Soldiers' Club

Palestine Lines of Communication

Ordnance Stores

32nd Combined Clearing Hospital

Motor Transport Lorries

Military Bakery

Motor Transport Tractors

Bethlehem Road watering area

to the coast broad gauge railway

Bethlehem Road

Royal Air Force Landing Ground

Desorps Military Camp

0 yards 400
0 metres 400

⊙ British military camps and installations, 1918.

'The Jewish problem, as seen in Jerusalem, is one of living interest, as there the visitor will see crowded into a few square miles samples, as it were, of that scatter-ed race from all the lands whence they have been driven, all drawn to their ancient Zion. He will realize, as probably he can never do in any other place, that stirring of the whole race Zionwards which seems to be on the eve of fulfilment, a consummation of the dreams of Jewish idealists through the long centuries of their dispersion'.

DR E.W. MASTERMAN
'THE DELIVERANCE OF JERUSALEM'
1918

© Martin Gilbert 1977

Map 35

Plate 55   The animal market at the Sultan's Pool, a photograph taken in 1910. The pool, formerly a Roman, Byzantine, Crusader, and Ottoman water reservoir, had long since been unable to serve the City's needs. Above it (left) is the British Ophthalmic Hospital, and (right), the Montefiore Houses of Shelter, 'Mishkenot Shaananim'. Since 1976 the Pool has been turned into a public garden, part of The Mitchell Garden (see Map 60).

Plate 56   A train arrives at Jerusalem Station in December 1917, when the railway was still narrow gauge, bringing with it soldiers of the Jewish Battalion of the British forces — the first Jewish military formation to enter Jerusalem since Roman times.

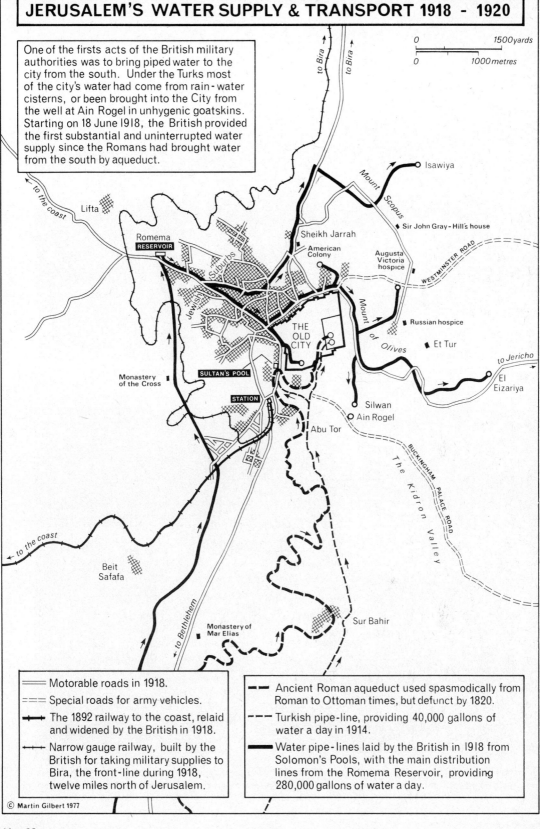

JERUSALEM'S WATER SUPPLY & TRANSPORT 1918 - 1920

One of the firsts acts of the British military authorities was to bring piped water to the city from the south. Under the Turks most of the city's water had come from rain-water cisterns, or been brought into the City from the well at Ain Rogel in unhygenic goatskins. Starting on 18 June 1918, the British provided the first substantial and uninterrupted water supply since the Romans had brought water from the south by aqueduct.

0   1500 yards
0   1000 metres

to Bira
to Bira
to the coast
Lifta
Isawiya
Mount Scopus
Sir John Gray - Hill's house
Sheikh Jarrah
American Colony
Augusta Victoria hospice
WESTMINSTER ROAD
Romema
RESERVOIR
Suburbs
Jewish
Russian hospice
Mount of Olives
Et Tur
THE OLD CITY
to Jericho
El Eizariya
Monastery of the Cross
SULTAN'S POOL
STATION
Silwan
Ain Rogel
Abu Tor
BUCKINGHAM PALACE ROAD
The Kidron Valley
to the coast
Beit Safafa
to Bethlehem
Monastery of Mar Elias
Sur Bahir

Motorable roads in 1918.

Special roads for army vehicles.

The 1892 railway to the coast, relaid and widened by the British in 1918.

Narrow gauge railway, built by the British for taking military supplies to Bira, the front-line during 1918, twelve miles north of Jerusalem.

Ancient Roman aqueduct used spasmodically from Roman to Ottoman times, but defunct by 1820.

Turkish pipe-line, providing 40,000 gallons of water a day in 1914.

Water pipe-lines laid by the British in 1918 from Solomon's Pools, with the main distribution lines from the Romema Reservoir, providing 280,000 gallons of water a day.

© Martin Gilbert 1977

Map 36

67

Plate 57 Mount Scopus in 1939 showing the British Military Cemetery (centre foreground), the Hadassah Hospital (left), part of the Hebrew University (right) and, appearing behind the Hebrew University building, the top of the Augusta-Victoria tower.

Plate 58 1950: an Israeli convoy sets off in the early morning from the Mandelbaum Gate on its fortnightly journey across Jordanian-held Jerusalem to the Israeli enclave on Mount Scopus.

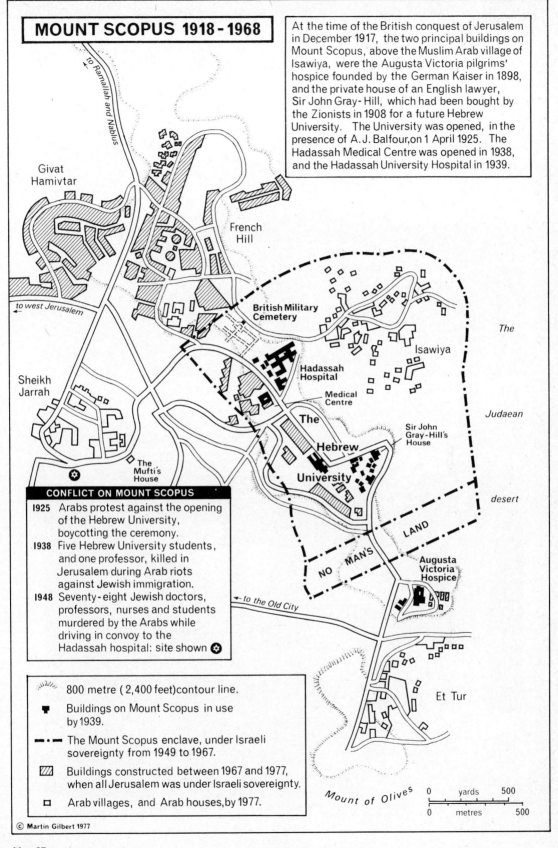

MOUNT SCOPUS 1918-1968

At the time of the British conquest of Jerusalem in December 1917, the two principal buildings on Mount Scopus, above the Muslim Arab village of Isawiya, were the Augusta Victoria pilgrims' hospice founded by the German Kaiser in 1898, and the private house of an English lawyer, Sir John Gray-Hill, which had been bought by the Zionists in 1908 for a future Hebrew University. The University was opened, in the presence of A.J. Balfour, on 1 April 1925. The Hadassah Medical Centre was opened in 1938, and the Hadassah University Hospital in 1939.

to Ramallah and Nablus

Givat Hamivtar

French Hill

to west Jerusalem

Sheikh Jarrah

British Military Cemetery

Isawiya

The

Hadassah Hospital

Medical Centre

Judaean

Sir John Gray-Hill's House

The Hebrew University

desert

The Mufti's House

CONFLICT ON MOUNT SCOPUS

1925 Arabs protest against the opening of the Hebrew University, boycotting the ceremony.

1938 Five Hebrew University students, and one professor, killed in Jerusalem during Arab riots against Jewish immigration.

1948 Seventy-eight Jewish doctors, professors, nurses and students murdered by the Arabs while driving in convoy to the Hadassah hospital: site shown ✿

NO MAN'S LAND

Augusta Victoria Hospice

to the Old City

Et Tur

〰️ 800 metre (2,400 feet) contour line.

▪ Buildings on Mount Scopus in use by 1939.

▬·▬·▬ The Mount Scopus enclave, under Israeli sovereignty from 1949 to 1967.

▨ Buildings constructed between 1967 and 1977, when all Jerusalem was under Israeli sovereignty.

▫ Arab villages, and Arab houses, by 1977.

© Martin Gilbert 1977

Mount of Olives

0   yards   500

0   metres   500

Map 37

Plate 59 A Zeppelin flies over the newly built King David Hotel. The first Zeppelin flew over Jerusalem on 26 March 1929, when it parachuted mailbags with letters from Germany. One of the bags was never found, and had probably been stolen. As a result, for future flights, a handbill was distributed which stated: "Keep your eye on the Zeppelin! Today the Zeppelin will pass over Palestine. The Zeppelin will drop mail-bags . . . whoever brings an undamaged bag will get the reward of 25 shillings . . ."

Plate 60 The Jerusalem Railway Station during the Mandate. With changes at Lydda Junction, one could travel by train not only to Tel Aviv and Haifa, but also to both Cairo and Damascus.

JERUSALEM AND THE BRITISH MANDATE 1922 - 1948

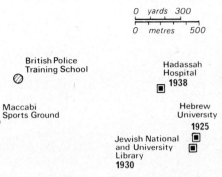

■ New buildings and institutes established during the British Mandate, with date of opening.

⌀ Other buildings of the Mandate period.

A British civil administration was set up in Jerusalem on 1 July 1920, and continued until 14 May 1948. The British League of Nations Mandate came into effect in 1922. Under British rule, both Jewish and Arab immigration to the City flourished: an extra 40,000 Jews and 20,000 Arabs settled in the city between 1931 and 1944. From 1921 the Jewish National Council, and from 1929 the Jewish Agency, both based in Jerusalem, worked within the terms of the British Mandate to establish a Jewish National Home in Palestine, and many new Jewish institutions were founded in the city. 75% of the City's taxpayers were Jews, but the City had only Arab Mayors from 1920 until 1944. A Muslim Supreme Council was established in 1921, a Higher Arab Committee in 1936.

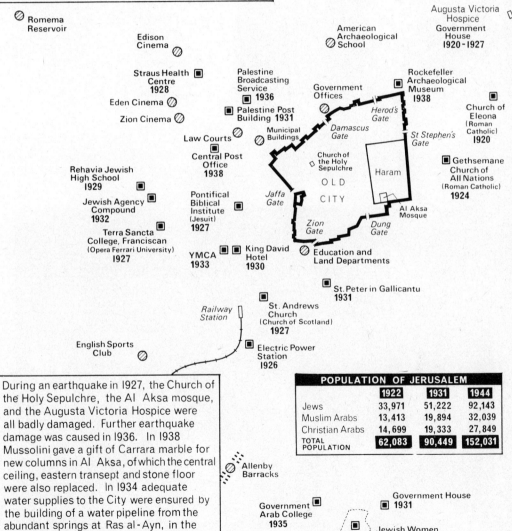

British Police Training School

Hadassah Hospital 1938

Maccabi Sports Ground

Hebrew University 1925

Jewish National and University Library 1930

Romema Reservoir

Augusta Victoria Hospice

Edison Cinema

American Archaeological School

Government House 1920-1927

Straus Health Centre 1928

Palestine Broadcasting Service 1936

Government Offices

Rockefeller Archaeological Museum 1938

Church of Eleona (Roman Catholic) 1920

Eden Cinema

Palestine Post Building 1931

Herod's Gate

Zion Cinema

Municipal Buildings

Damascus Gate

St Stephen's Gate

Law Courts

Central Post Office 1938

Church of the Holy Sepulchre

Haram

Gethsemane Church of All Nations (Roman Catholic) 1924

Rehavia Jewish High School 1929

OLD

Jewish Agency Compound 1932

Pontifical Biblical Institute (Jesuit) 1927

Jaffa Gate

CITY

Al Aksa Mosque

Terra Sancta College, Franciscan (Opera Ferrari University) 1927

Zion Gate

Dung Gate

YMCA 1933

King David Hotel 1930

Education and Land Departments

St. Peter in Gallicantu 1931

Railway Station

St. Andrews Church (Church of Scotland) 1927

English Sports Club

Electric Power Station 1926

During an earthquake in 1927, the Church of the Holy Sepulchre, the Al Aksa mosque, and the Augusta Victoria Hospice were all badly damaged. Further earthquake damage was caused in 1936. In 1938 Mussolini gave a gift of Carrara marble for new columns in Al Aksa, of which the central ceiling, eastern transept and stone floor were also replaced. In 1934 adequate water supplies to the City were ensured by the building of a water pipeline from the abundant springs at Ras al-Ayn, in the coastal plain, to the Romema Reservoir.

POPULATION OF JERUSALEM			
	1922	1931	1944
Jews	33,971	51,222	92,143
Muslim Arabs	13,413	19,894	32,039
Christian Arabs	14,699	19,333	27,849
TOTAL POPULATION	62,083	90,449	152,031

Allenby Barracks

Government Arab College 1935

Government House 1931

Jewish Women Workers Farm 1920

© Martin Gilbert 1977

Map 38

Plate 61   Milk Delivery in the Old City; a photograph taken in the mid-1920s.

Plate 62   Light Industry: a Jewish workshop, photographed by Josef Zweig on 23 March 1926.

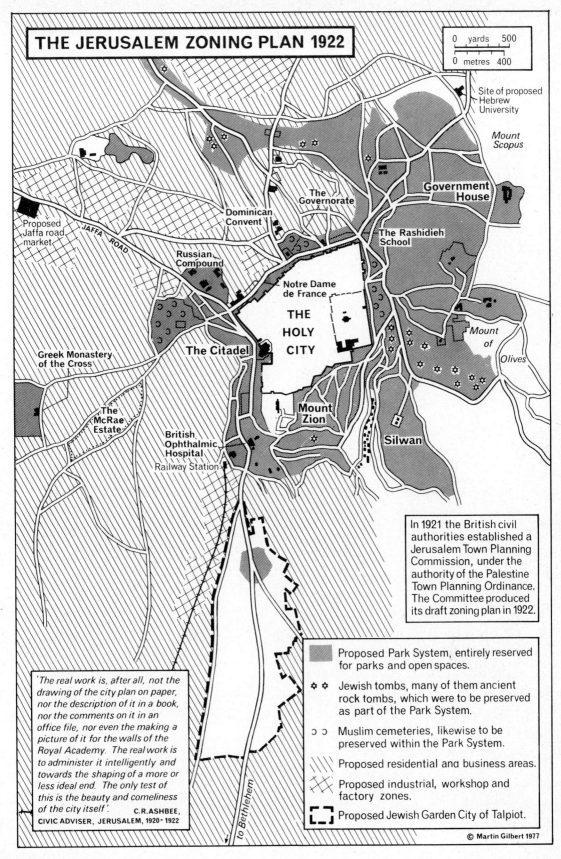

THE JERUSALEM ZONING PLAN 1922

0 yards 500
0 metres 400

Site of proposed Hebrew University

Mount Scopus

Government House

Proposed Jaffa road market

JAFFA ROAD

The Governorate

Dominican Convent

The Rashidieh School

Russian Compound

Notre Dame de France

THE HOLY CITY

Greek Monastery of the Cross

The Citadel

Mount of Olives

The McRae Estate

Mount Zion

Silwan

British Ophthalmic Hospital

Railway Station

In 1921 the British civil authorities established a Jerusalem Town Planning Commission, under the authority of the Palestine Town Planning Ordinance. The Committee produced its draft zoning plan in 1922.

'The real work is, after all, not the drawing of the city plan on paper, nor the description of it in a book, nor the comments on it in an office file, nor even the making a picture of it for the walls of the Royal Academy. The real work is to administer it intelligently and towards the shaping of a more or less ideal end. The only test of this is the beauty and comeliness of the city itself'. C.R.ASHBEE, CIVIC ADVISER, JERUSALEM, 1920-1922

to Bethlehem

Proposed Park System, entirely reserved for parks and open spaces.

Jewish tombs, many of them ancient rock tombs, which were to be preserved as part of the Park System.

Muslim cemeteries, likewise to be preserved within the Park System.

Proposed residential and business areas.

Proposed industrial, workshop and factory zones.

Proposed Jewish Garden City of Talpiot.

© Martin Gilbert 1977

Map 39

73

Plate 63   The site chosen for Boneh Bayit Garden City, later Bet Hakerem. A photograph taken in 1922.

Plate 64   Bet Hakerem Garden City; a photograph taken in May 1937.

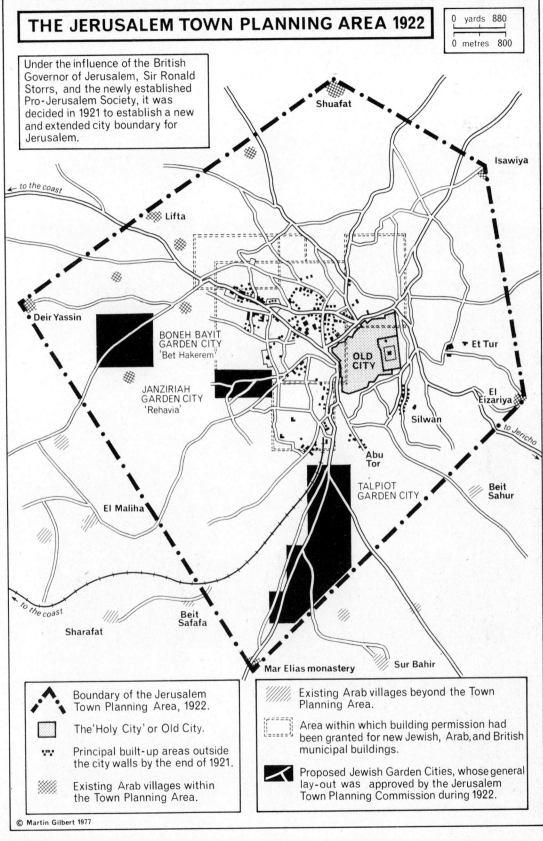

THE JERUSALEM TOWN PLANNING AREA 1922

0 yards 880
0 metres 800

Under the influence of the British Governor of Jerusalem, Sir Ronald Storrs, and the newly established Pro-Jerusalem Society, it was decided in 1921 to establish a new and extended city boundary for Jerusalem.

Shuafat

Isawiya

← to the coast

Lifta

Deir Yassin

BONEH BAYIT
GARDEN CITY
'Bet Hakerem'

JANZIRIAH
GARDEN CITY
'Rehavia'

OLD
CITY

Et Tur

El
Eizariya

Silwan

to Jericho

Abu
Tor

El Maliha

TALPIOT
GARDEN CITY

Beit
Sahur

← to the coast

Beit
Safafa

Sharafat

Mar Elias monastery   Sur Bahir

Boundary of the Jerusalem Town Planning Area, 1922.

The 'Holy City' or Old City.

Principal built-up areas outside the city walls by the end of 1921.

Existing Arab villages within the Town Planning Area.

Existing Arab villages beyond the Town Planning Area.

Area within which building permission had been granted for new Jewish, Arab, and British municipal buildings.

Proposed Jewish Garden Cities, whose general lay-out was approved by the Jerusalem Town Planning Commission during 1922.

© Martin Gilbert 1977

Map 40

75

Plate 65   Building a suburb. Rehavia, the first phase, 1921.

Plate 66   A suburb in being: Rehavia in 1937.

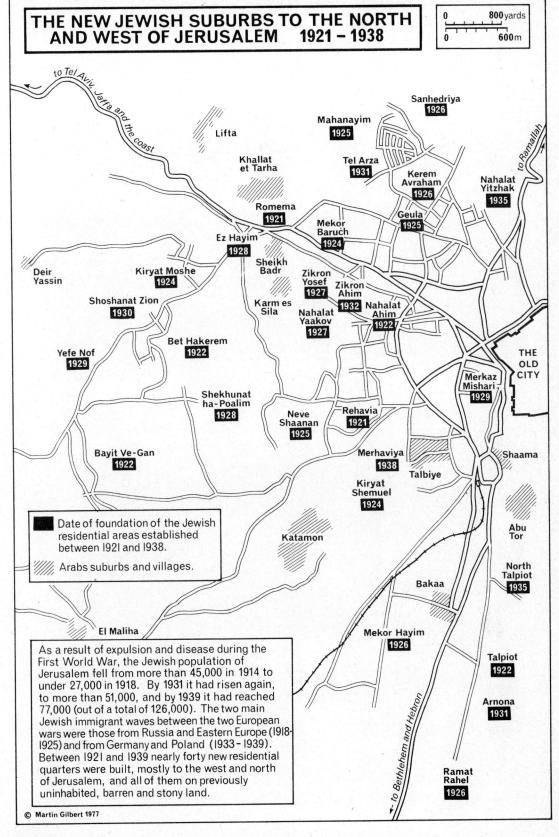

THE NEW JEWISH SUBURBS TO THE NORTH AND WEST OF JERUSALEM   1921 – 1938

0 ____ 800 yards
0 ____ 600m

to Tel Aviv Jaffa and the coast

Lifta

Sanhedriya
1926

Mahanayim
1925

Khallat et Tarha

Tel Arza
1931

Kerem Avraham
1926

Nahalat Yitzhak
1935

Romema
1921

Mekor Baruch
1924

Geula
1925

to Ramallah

Ez Hayim
1928

Sheikh Badr

Deir Yassin

Kiryat Moshe
1924

Zikron Yosef
1927

Zikron Ahim
1932

Nahalat Ahim
1922

Shoshanat Zion
1930

Karm es Sila

Nahalat Yaakov
1927

Yefe Nof
1929

Bet Hakerem
1922

THE OLD CITY

Shekhunat ha-Poalim
1928

Neve Shaanan
1925

Rehavia
1921

Merkaz Mishari
1929

Bayit Ve-Gan
1922

Merhaviya
1938

Talbiye

Shaama

Kiryat Shemuel
1924

Abu Tor

Katamon

North Talpiot
1935

Bakaa

El Maliha

Mekor Hayim
1926

Talpiot
1922

Arnona
1931

to Bethlehem and Hebron

Ramat Rahel
1926

■ Date of foundation of the Jewish residential areas established between 1921 and 1938.

▨ Arabs suburbs and villages.

As a result of expulsion and disease during the First World War, the Jewish population of Jerusalem fell from more than 45,000 in 1914 to under 27,000 in 1918. By 1931 it had risen again, to more than 51,000, and by 1939 it had reached 77,000 (out of a total of 126,000). The two main Jewish immigrant waves between the two European wars were those from Russia and Eastern Europe (1918-1925) and from Germany and Poland (1933–1939). Between 1921 and 1939 nearly forty new residential quarters were built, mostly to the west and north of Jerusalem, and all of them on previously uninhabited, barren and stony land.

© Martin Gilbert 1977

Map 41   77

Plate 67 Jerusalem 8 April 1933. Zionist leaders, including Dr. Weizmann and Chaim Arlozoroff (front row, with glasses) meet Arab leaders from Transjordan at the King David Hotel, in an attempt to reconcile Arab-Jewish differences.

Plate 68 Jewish residents flee from the Old City during the Arab riots of 1936.

JERUSALEM, ZIONISM AND THE ARAB REVOLT 1920-1940

///// Built up areas of Jerusalem by 1938.

—— Jewish bus routes.

--- Arab bus routes.

■ Jewish suburbs attacked and looted in 1929; nearly 4,000 Jews were forced to leave their homes.

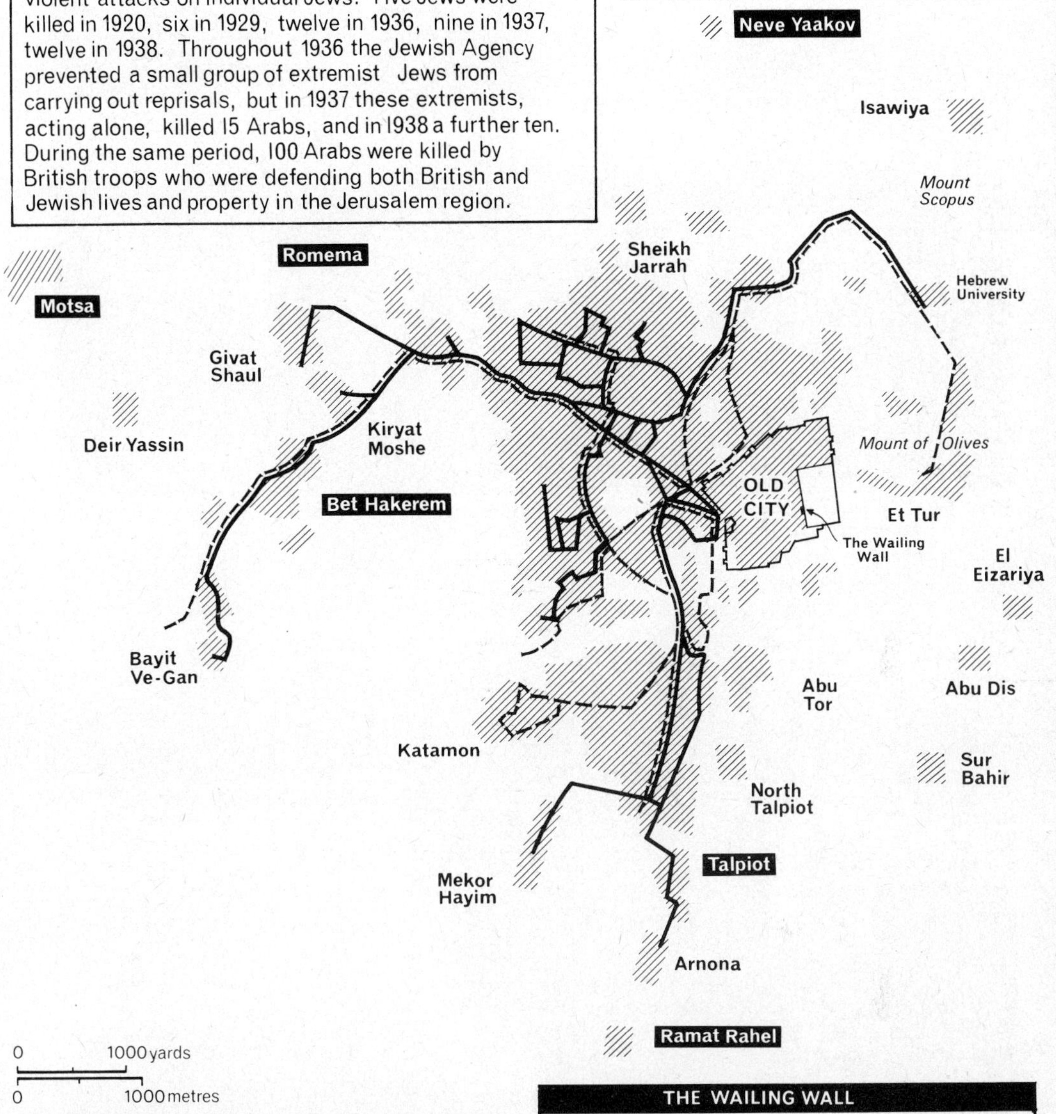

Between 1920 and 1940 Arab hostility towards Jewish immigration, and towards the Jewish presence in Jerusalem (a majority presence since the 1860s) was inflamed by agitators and fanatics, and led to many violent attacks on individual Jews. Five Jews were killed in 1920, six in 1929, twelve in 1936, nine in 1937, twelve in 1938. Throughout 1936 the Jewish Agency prevented a small group of extremist Jews from carrying out reprisals, but in 1937 these extremists, acting alone, killed 15 Arabs, and in 1938 a further ten. During the same period, 100 Arabs were killed by British troops who were defending both British and Jewish lives and property in the Jerusalem region.

Neve Yaakov

Isawiya

Mount Scopus

Romema

Sheikh Jarrah

Hebrew University

Motsa

Givat Shaul

Kiryat Moshe

Deir Yassin

Bet Hakerem

Mount of Olives

OLD CITY

Et Tur

The Wailing Wall

El Eizariya

Bayit Ve-Gan

Abu Tor

Abu Dis

Katamon

Sur Bahir

North Talpiot

Talpiot

Mekor Hayim

Arnona

Ramat Rahel

0   1000 yards

0   1000 metres

THE WAILING WALL

In 1929, after Arab attacks on individual Jews praying at the Wall, and a Jewish demonstration at the Wall with the Zionist flag and anthem, a crowd of 2,000 Muslim Arabs destroyed prayer books at the Wall, injured the beadle, and attacked Jews throughout the city, killing six Jews including a Rabbi and two children in the suburb of Motsa. In Hebron 59 Jews were killed, in Safed 20, in Tel Aviv 6, elsewhere in Palestine 42.

© Martin Gilbert 1977

Map 42

79

Plate 69   1936: Arab schoolgirls march with their headmistress, Hind Husseini, during widespread Arab demonstrations against Jewish immigration into Palestine.

Plate 70   18 May 1939: Jewish veterans, former soldiers in the British Army, demonstrate against the Palestine White Paper of May 1939. At a time of growing Nazi persecution of Jews in Germany, Austria and Czechoslovakia, the White Paper imposed a strict limitation on all future Jewish immigration, and was designed, following Arab pressures, to prevent any future Jewish majority in Palestine.

JEWISH AND ARAB IMMIGRATION TO JERUSALEM 1922 - 1939

With the initial security and stability provided by British rule and the British Mandate, and with the prosperity introduced by Zionist enterprises, both Jews and Arabs migrated to Jerusalem in large numbers between the wars. Repeated Arab demonstrations, many of them violent, led to the British Government's White Paper of May 1939, restricting Jewish immigration to a maximum of 75,000 by 1945, and giving the Arabs a veto on all Jewish immigration after 1945.

British census returns show that between 1922 and 1931 the population of the Jerusalem Sub-District rose from 91,272 to 132,661, an increase of 41,389; and that this increase, consisting largely by immigration from abroad, was made up, according to the census returns, made up, of more than 20,000 Jews, and over 21,000 Arabs.

Five separate Arab States had pressed Britain to restrict Jewish immigration in 1939: Egypt, Iraq, Transjordan, Saudi Arabia and Yemen.

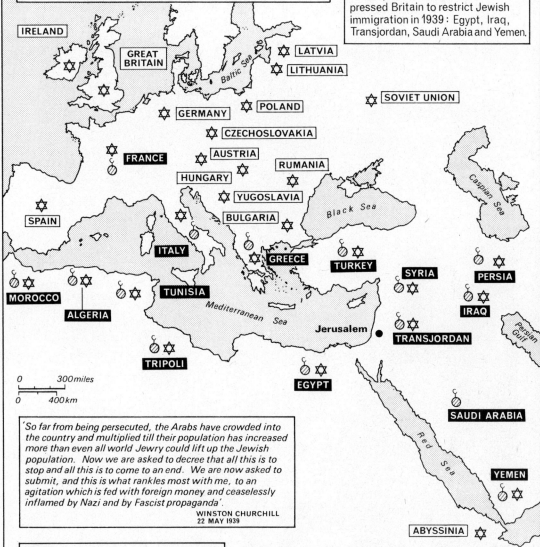

'So far from being persecuted, the Arabs have crowded into the country and multiplied till their population has increased more than even all world Jewry could lift up the Jewish population. Now we are asked to decree that all this is to stop and all this is to come to an end. We are now asked to submit, and this is what rankles most with me, to an agitation which is fed with foreign money and ceaselessly inflamed by Nazi and by Fascist propaganda'.

WINSTON CHURCHILL
22 MAY 1939

■ Countries from which both Arabs and Jews emigrated, 1922 - 1931, to settle in Jerusalem.

□ Countries from which Jews alone emigrated, 1922 - 1931, to settle in Jerusalem.

Between 1931 and 1939 the Jewish population of the City of Jerusalem rose by a further 26,000, while the Arab population rose by a further 15,000. Most of the Jewish and Arab immigrants came from the countries shown on this map; the Jews principally from Poland and Germany, the Arabs mostly from Syria and Transjordan.

Map 43

Plate 71 The Jewish Quarter of the Old City in 1937, with the domes of two of the synagogues. To the left, the Mount of Olives.

Plate 72 Ben Yehuda Street, one of the main shopping streets in the centre of the predominantly Jewish area of the city; a photograph taken in 1935.

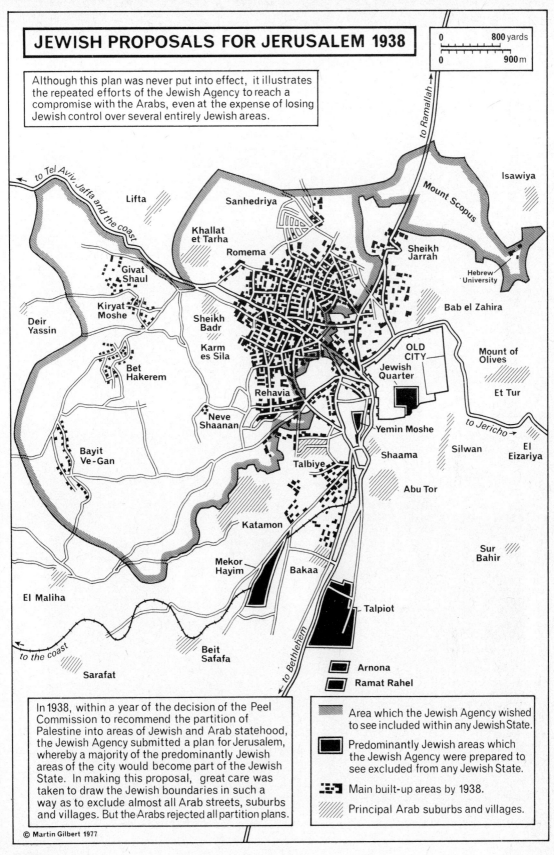

JEWISH PROPOSALS FOR JERUSALEM 1938

0 ____ 800 yards
0 ____ 900 m

Although this plan was never put into effect, it illustrates the repeated efforts of the Jewish Agency to reach a compromise with the Arabs, even at the expense of losing Jewish control over several entirely Jewish areas.

to Ramallah

to Tel Aviv, Jaffa and the coast

Isawiya

Lifta

Sanhedriya

Mount Scopus

Khallat et Tarha

Romema

Sheikh Jarrah

Givat Shaul

Hebrew University

Kiryat Moshe

Deir Yassin

Sheikh Badr

Bab el Zahira

Karm es Sila

OLD CITY

Mount of Olives

Bet Hakerem

Jewish Quarter

Rehavia

Et Tur

Neve Shaanan

Yemin Moshe

Bayit Ve-Gan

Shaama

Silwan

El Eizariya

to Jericho

Talbiye

Abu Tor

Katamon

Sur Bahir

Mekor Hayim

Bakaa

El Maliha

Talpiot

to the coast

Beit Safafa

to Bethlehem

Arnona

Sarafat

Ramat Rahel

In 1938, within a year of the decision of the Peel Commission to recommend the partition of Palestine into areas of Jewish and Arab statehood, the Jewish Agency submitted a plan for Jerusalem, whereby a majority of the predominantly Jewish areas of the city would become part of the Jewish State. In making this proposal, great care was taken to draw the Jewish boundaries in such a way as to exclude almost all Arab streets, suburbs and villages. But the Arabs rejected all partition plans.

Area which the Jewish Agency wished to see included within any Jewish State.

Predominantly Jewish areas which the Jewish Agency were prepared to see excluded from any Jewish State.

Main built-up areas by 1938.

Principal Arab suburbs and villages.

© Martin Gilbert 1977

Map 44

83

Plate 73   An Arab family in their Katamon home. A photograph taken by the Swedish photographer Anna Riwkin in 1946.

Plate 74   Arab women and Orthodox Jews; a photograph taken by Anna Riwkin in 1946.

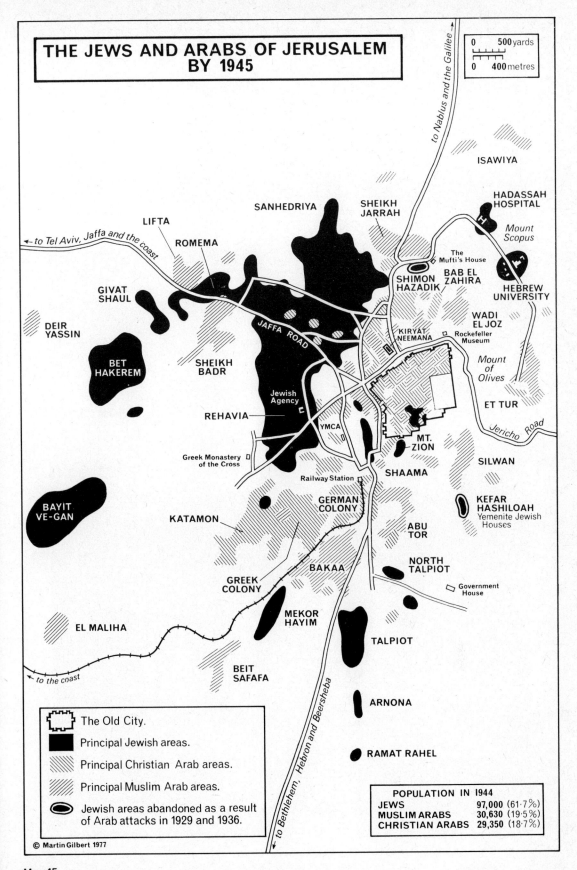

THE JEWS AND ARABS OF JERUSALEM
BY 1945

| 0 | 500 | yards |
| 0 | 400 | metres |

to Nablus and the Galilee

ISAWIYA

← to Tel Aviv, Jaffa and the coast

LIFTA

ROMEMA

SANHEDRIYA

SHEIKH JARRAH

HADASSAH HOSPITAL

Mount Scopus

The Mufti's House

SHIMON HAZADIK

BAB EL ZAHIRA

HEBREW UNIVERSITY

GIVAT SHAUL

DEIR YASSIN

JAFFA ROAD

WADI EL JOZ

BET HAKEREM

SHEIKH BADR

KIRYAT NEEMANA

Rockefeller Museum

Mount of Olives

Jewish Agency

REHAVIA

YMCA

ET TUR

Jericho Road

Greek Monastery of the Cross

MT. ZION

SILWAN

BAYIT VE-GAN

Railway Station

SHAAMA

KATAMON

GERMAN COLONY

ABU TOR

KEFAR HASHILOAH
Yemenite Jewish Houses

BAKAA

NORTH TALPIOT

GREEK COLONY

Government House

EL MALIHA

MEKOR HAYIM

TALPIOT

BEIT SAFAFA

ARNONA

← to the coast

to Bethlehem, Hebron and Beersheba

RAMAT RAHEL

The Old City.

Principal Jewish areas.

Principal Christian Arab areas.

Principal Muslim Arab areas.

Jewish areas abandoned as a result of Arab attacks in 1929 and 1936.

© Martin Gilbert 1977

POPULATION IN 1944	
JEWS	97,000 (61·7%)
MUSLIM ARABS	30,630 (19·5%)
CHRISTIAN ARABS	29,350 (18·7%)

Map 45

85

Plate 75   The King David Hotel in July 1947, after the Jewish terrorist attack.

Plate 76   Princess Mary Street in April 1948, when it was one of the borders of a British security zone.

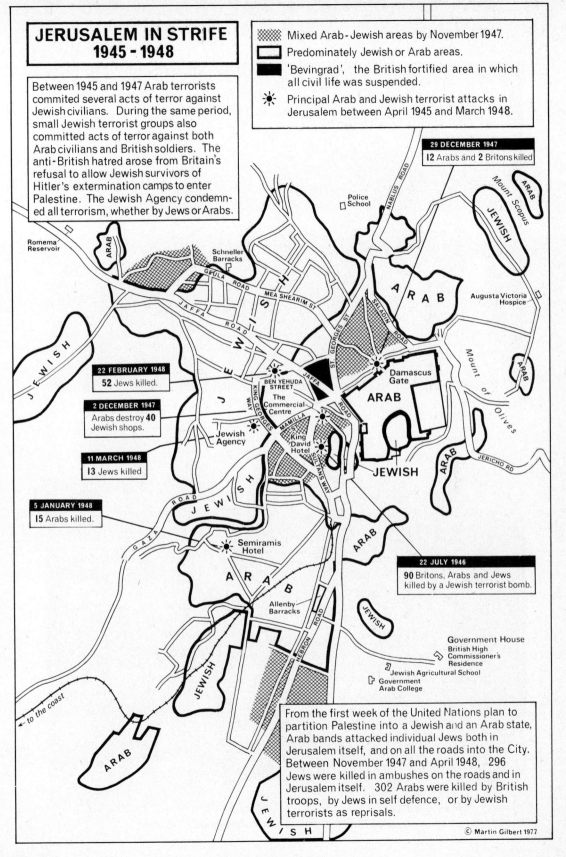

JERUSALEM IN STRIFE 1945 - 1948

Mixed Arab - Jewish areas by November 1947.

Predominately Jewish or Arab areas.

'Bevingrad', the British fortified area in which all civil life was suspended.

Principal Arab and Jewish terrorist attacks in Jerusalem between April 1945 and March 1948.

Between 1945 and 1947 Arab terrorists commited several acts of terror against Jewish civilians. During the same period, small Jewish terrorist groups also committed acts of terror against both Arab civilians and British soldiers. The anti-British hatred arose from Britain's refusal to allow Jewish survivors of Hitler's extermination camps to enter Palestine. The Jewish Agency condemned all terrorism, whether by Jews or Arabs.

29 DECEMBER 1947
12 Arabs and 2 Britons killed

Romema Reservoir

Police School

Mount Scopus ARAB JEWISH

Schneller Barracks

GEULA ROAD

MEA SHEARIM ST

NABLUS ROAD

Augusta Victoria Hospice

JAFFA ROAD

ST. GEORGES ST

SALADIN ROAD

A R A B

JEWISH

22 FEBRUARY 1948
52 Jews killed.

BEN YEHUDA STREET
The Commercial Centre

JAFFA ROAD

Damascus Gate

ARAB

Mount of Olives

2 DECEMBER 1947
Arabs destroy 40 Jewish shops.

KING GEORGES WAY

MAMILLA
King David Hotel

Jewish Agency

SULTAN'S WAY

ARAB

JEWISH

JERICHO RD

11 MARCH 1948
13 Jews killed

J E W I S H

GAZA ROAD

5 JANUARY 1948
15 Arabs killed.

Semiramis Hotel

A R A B

ARAB

JEWISH

22 JULY 1946
90 Britons, Arabs and Jews killed by a Jewish terrorist bomb.

Allenby Barracks

HEBRON ROAD

JEWISH

Government House
British High Commissioner's Residence
Jewish Agricultural School
Government Arab College

ARAB

← to the coast

ARAB

From the first week of the United Nations plan to partition Palestine into a Jewish and an Arab state, Arab bands attacked individual Jews both in Jerusalem itself, and on all the roads into the City. Between November 1947 and April 1948, 296 Jews were killed in ambushes on the roads and in Jerusalem itself. 302 Arabs were killed by British troops, by Jews in self defence, or by Jewish terrorists as reprisals.

JEWISH

© Martin Gilbert 1977

Map 46

Plate 77   Arab Volunteers, a photograph taken by Hanna Safieh in 1948.

Plate 78   A Jewish truck, attacked by Arab Volunteers on the Bethlehem Road, 1948.

JEWISH AND ARAB SUBURBS IN THE JERUSALEM AREA BY 1947

By 1947 there were eighteen Jewish settlements within fifteen miles of Jerusalem, two of which, Har Tuv and Motsa, had been founded in 1895, the rest between 1920 and 1947. A further two settlements had been abandoned as a result of Arab attacks in 1929 and 1936, one of them the Jewish community of Hebron, which dated from ancient times.

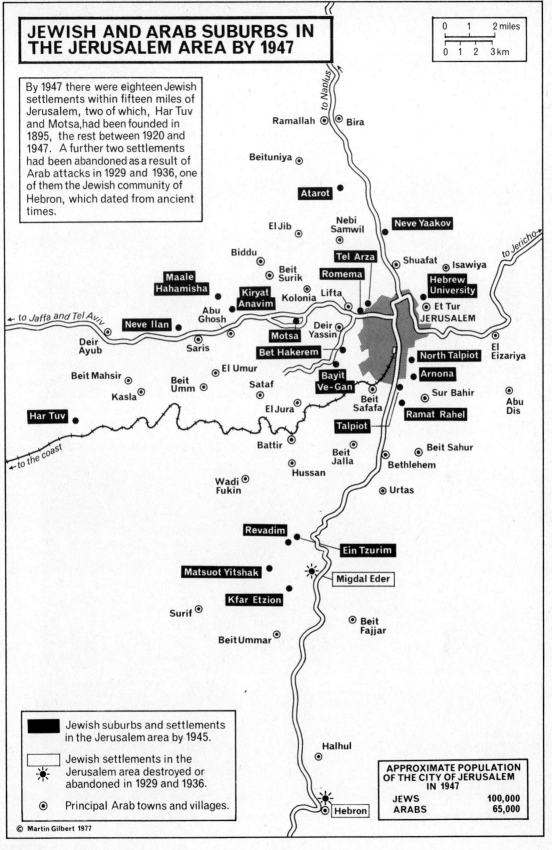

```
                                                0   1    2 miles
                                                0  1  2  3 km
```

to Naplus

Ramallah ⊙   ⊙ Bira

Beituniya ⊙

Atarot

El Jib ⊙   Nebi
               Samwil   **Neve Yaakov**
                  ⊙
Biddu   Shuafat ⊙   ⊙ Isawiya
    ⊙   Beit   **Tel Arza**   to Jericho
         Surik ⊙ **Romema**   **Hebrew**
Maale   ⊙ Kolonia Lifta   **University**
Hahamisha **Kiryat**   ⊙ Et Tur
         Anavim   JERUSALEM
← to Jaffa and Tel Aviv Abu   El Eizariya
         Ghosh   ⊙
Neve Ilan ⊙   Deir
Deir   Saris **Motsa** Yassin ⊙   **North Talpiot**
Ayub   ⊙   **Bet Hakerem**   **Arnona**
                                              ⊙ Sur Bahir
Beit Mahsir ⊙   El Umur ⊙ Sataf **Bayit**   Abu
        Beit   **Ve-Gan** Beit   **Ramat Rahel** Dis
Kasla ⊙ Umm ⊙   El Jura   Safafa   ⊙
Har Tuv   **Talpiot**
                   Battir ⊙   ⊙ Beit Sahur
← to the coast   Beit   Bethlehem ⊙
                              Jalla ⊙
          Wadi ⊙   ⊙ Urtas
          Fukin   Hussan

                  Revadim
                         Ein Tzurim
      Matsuot Yitshak   ☀ **Migdal Eder**
         Kfar Etzion
   Surif ⊙   ⊙ Beit
   Beit Ummar ⊙   Fajjar

                         Halhul ⊙
```

**Legend:**

■ Jewish suburbs and settlements in the Jerusalem area by 1945.

☀ Jewish settlements in the Jerusalem area destroyed or abandoned in 1929 and 1936.

⊙ Principal Arab towns and villages.

| APPROXIMATE POPULATION OF THE CITY OF JERUSALEM IN 1947 | |
| --- | --- |
| JEWS | 100,000 |
| ARABS | 65,000 |

☀ ⊙ **Hebron**

© Martin Gilbert 1977

Map 47

89
```

Plate 79   The Arab reaction to the United Nations vote in favour of two Palestine States, one Jewish and the other Arab; looting and burning Jerusalem's predominantly Jewish "Commercial Centre", 2 December 1947.

Plate 80   Arab terrorism continued: the Ben Yehuda Street explosion of 22 February 1948.

THE UNITED NATIONS' PLAN FOR JERUSALEM, 1947

On 29 November 1947, as part of its resolution on Palestine (RESOLUTION 181 (II) A), the General Assembly of the United Nations adopted the proposal that "The City of Jerusalem shall be established as a *corpus seperatum* under a special international régime and shall be administered by the United Nations". Under this plan, a referendum was to be held after ten years to seek the views of the City's residents as to whether the international régime should continue, or be modified.

POPULATION OF THE JERUSALEM MUNICIPALITY, 1947

Jews	99,320
Arabs	65,000

POPULATION OF THE 'SPECIAL INTERNATIONAL REGIME' AREA, AS DRAWN BY THE U.N.

Arabs	105,000
Jews	100,000

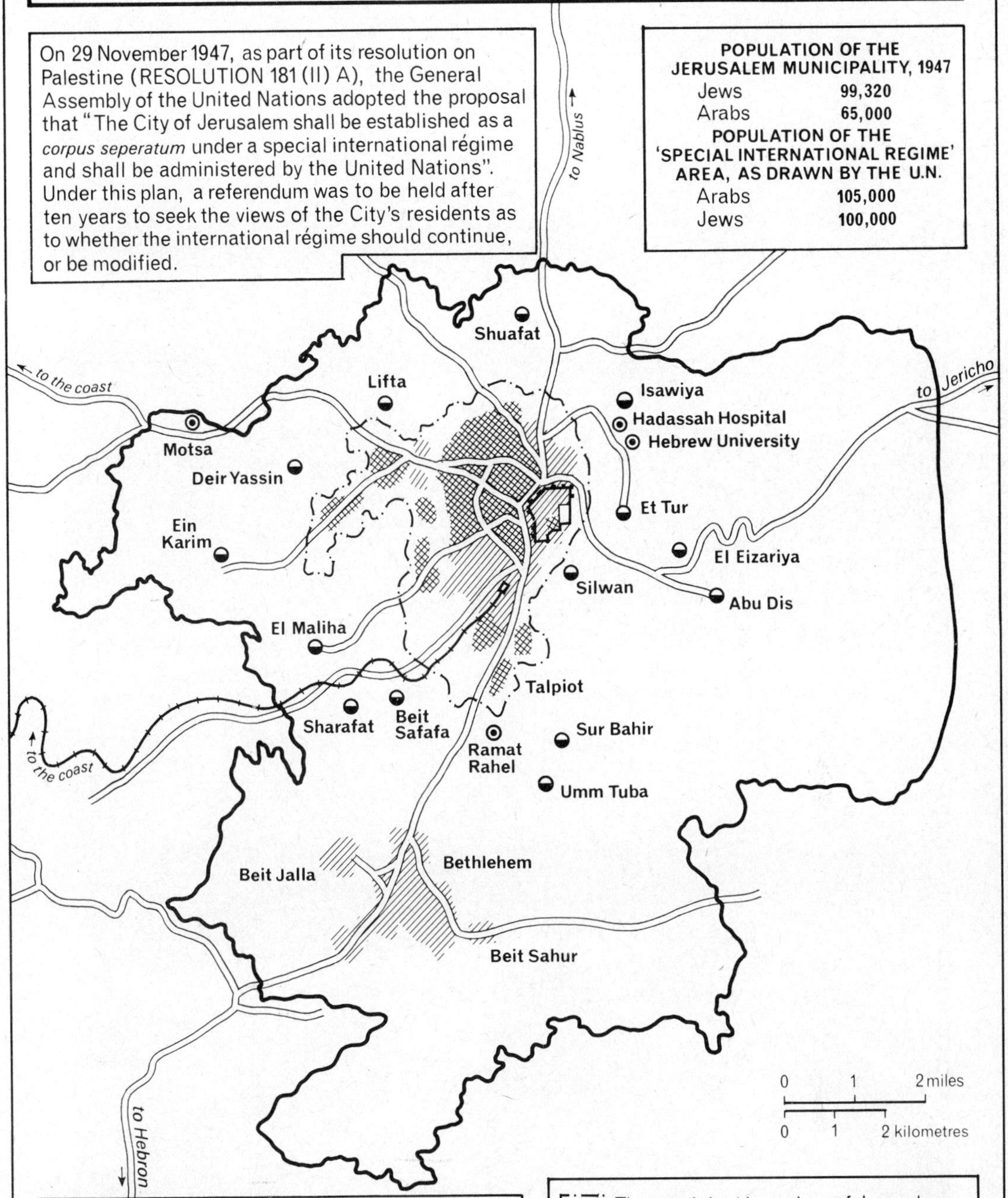

to Nablus

to the coast

to Jericho

Shuafat

Lifta

Isawiya

Hadassah Hospital

Hebrew University

Motsa

Deir Yassin

Et Tur

El Eizariya

Ein Karim

Silwan

Abu Dis

El Maliha

Talpiot

Sharafat

Beit Safafa

Sur Bahir

Ramat Rahel

Umm Tuba

to the coast

Beit Jalla

Bethlehem

Beit Sahur

to Hebron

| 0 | 1 | 2 miles |

| 0 | 1 | 2 kilometres |

The Jewish Agency accepted this plan, describing it as a "heavy sacrifice" which would nevertheless serve as "the Jewish contribution to the solution of a painful problem". The Arab Higher Committee, supported by Iraq, Saudi Arabia and Syria, rejected the plan, and called instead for a "unified independent Palestine". Although the United States and the Soviet Union both supported the plan, it was never put into effect.

The municipal boundary of Jerusalem in 1947, under the British Mandate.

Boundary of the "special international régime", as proposed by the U.N.

Principal Jewish suburbs within the proposed U.N. régime.

Principal Arab suburbs and villages within the proposed U.N. régime.

© Martin Gilbert 1977

Map 48

91

Plate 81 Scene of an Arab ambush at Bab el-Wad, on the road to Jerusalem, 1948. The trucks were left by the roadside as a memorial to the dead; a photograph taken in the 1960s.

Plate 82 A Jewish convoy reaches the outskirts of besieged Jerusalem, 1948.

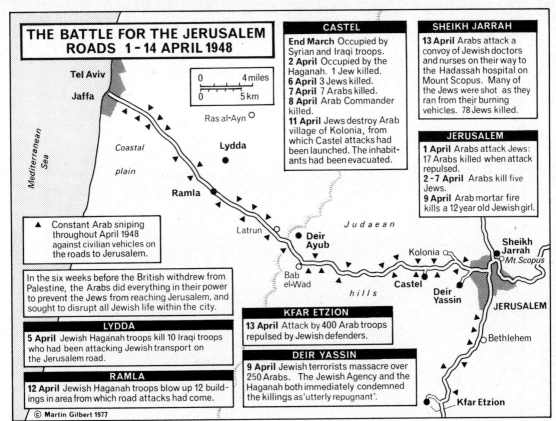

THE BATTLE FOR THE JERUSALEM ROADS 1 – 14 APRIL 1948

0 — 4 miles
0 — 5 km

▲ Constant Arab sniping throughout April 1948 against civilian vehicles on the roads to Jerusalem.

In the six weeks before the British withdrew from Palestine, the Arabs did everything in their power to prevent the Jews from reaching Jerusalem, and sought to disrupt all Jewish life within the city.

LYDDA
5 April Jewish Haganah troops kill 10 Iraqi troops who had been attacking Jewish transport on the Jerusalem road.

RAMLA
12 April Jewish Haganah troops blow up 12 buildings in area from which road attacks had come.

© Martin Gilbert 1977

CASTEL
End March Occupied by Syrian and Iraqi troops.
2 April Occupied by the Haganah. 1 Jew killed.
6 April 3 Jews killed.
7 April 7 Arabs killed.
8 April Arab Commander killed.
11 April Jews destroy Arab village of Kolonia, from which Castel attacks had been launched. The inhabitants had been evacuated.

SHEIKH JARRAH
13 April Arabs attack a convoy of Jewish doctors and nurses on their way to the Hadassah hospital on Mount Scopus. Many of the Jews were shot as they ran from their burning vehicles. 78 Jews killed.

JERUSALEM
1 April Arabs attack Jews: 17 Arabs killed when attack repulsed.
2 – 7 April Arabs kill five Jews.
9 April Arab mortar fire kills a 12 year old Jewish girl.

KFAR ETZION
13 April Attack by 400 Arab troops repulsed by Jewish defenders.

DEIR YASSIN
9 April Jewish terrorists massacre over 250 Arabs. The Jewish Agency and the Haganah both immediately condemned the killings as 'utterly repugnant'.

Map 49

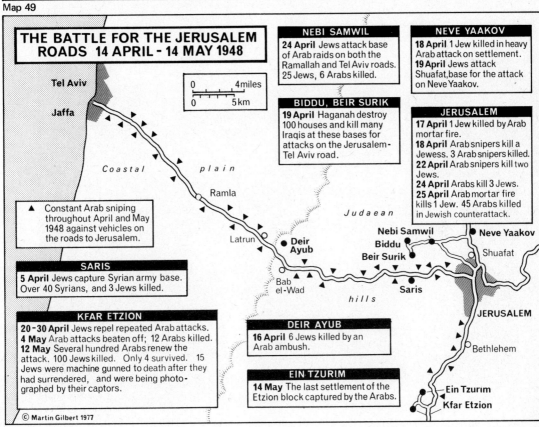

THE BATTLE FOR THE JERUSALEM ROADS 14 APRIL – 14 MAY 1948

0 — 4 miles
0 — 5 km

▲ Constant Arab sniping throughout April and May 1948 against vehicles on the roads to Jerusalem.

SARIS
5 April Jews capture Syrian army base. Over 40 Syrians, and 3 Jews killed.

KFAR ETZION
20 – 30 April Jews repel repeated Arab attacks.
4 May Arab attacks beaten off; 12 Arabs killed.
12 May Several hundred Arabs renew the attack. 100 Jews killed. Only 4 survived. 15 Jews were machine gunned to death after they had surrendered, and were being photographed by their captors.

© Martin Gilbert 1977

NEBI SAMWIL
24 April Jews attack base of Arab raids on both the Ramallah and Tel Aviv roads. 25 Jews, 6 Arabs killed.

BIDDU, BEIR SURIK
19 April Haganah destroy 100 houses and kill many Iraqis at these bases for attacks on the Jerusalem-Tel Aviv road.

DEIR AYUB
16 April 6 Jews killed by an Arab ambush.

EIN TZURIM
14 May The last settlement of the Etzion block captured by the Arabs.

NEVE YAAKOV
18 April 1 Jew killed in heavy Arab attack on settlement.
19 April Jews attack Shuafat, base for the attack on Neve Yaakov.

JERUSALEM
17 April 1 Jew killed by Arab mortar fire.
18 April Arab snipers kill a Jewess. 3 Arab snipers killed.
22 April Arab snipers kill two Jews.
24 April Arabs kill 3 Jews.
25 April Arab mortar fire kills 1 Jew. 45 Arabs killed in Jewish counterattack.

Map 50

Plate 83   The Jewish Agency building in Jerusalem, blown up by Arab terrorists on 11 March 1948, two months before the ending of British rule. Among the thirteen Jewish dead was the 72 year old Zionist writer and administrator, Leib Jaffe.

Plate 84   British soldiers, formerly stationed in Jerusalem, embark at Haifa, for Britain, on the steamship *Samaria,* May 1948.

JERUSALEM UNDER SIEGE 1948

On 15 May 1948, following the departure of all British troops from Jerusalem, three Arab armies - those of Egypt, Iraq and the Arab Legion from Transjordan - together with Syrian troops, surrounded Jerusalem, bombarded the City, and sought to capture it. In four weeks, 170 Jewish civilians were killed and 1,000 were injured by Arab shellfire. A truce was signed on 11 June 1948. On 7 July, at the end of the truce, Israeli forces captured Ein Kerem from the Egyptian forces holding it.

'During the last few weeks we have succeeded in substantially increasing our effective strength on land and in the air in all parts of the country. It is absolutely essential that Jewish Jerusalem shall continue to stand fast during these days of trial. Notwithstanding the end of the fighting in the Old City, strenuous efforts to relieve Jerusalem and its surroundings are in hand and being pressed.... Be strong and of good courage'.

DAVID BEN GURION,
MESSAGE TO JERUSALEM
30 MAY 1948

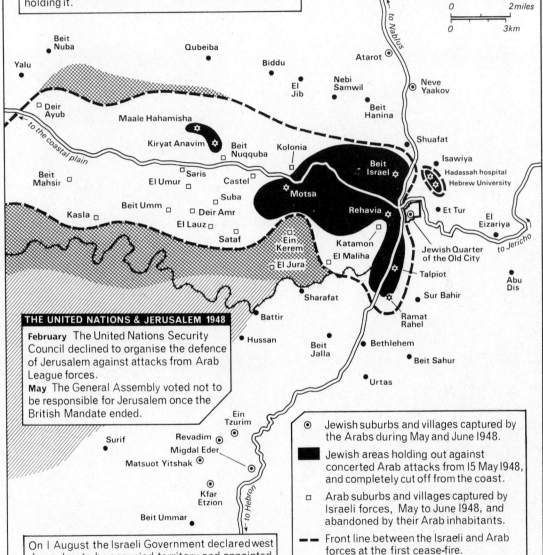

THE UNITED NATIONS & JERUSALEM 1948

February The United Nations Security Council declined to organise the defence of Jerusalem against attacks from Arab League forces.
May The General Assembly voted not to be responsible for Jerusalem once the British Mandate ended.

On 1 August the Israeli Government declared west Jerusalem to be occupied territory and appointed a Military Governor, Dov Joseph. On 17 September, following the assassination of the UN mediator, Count Bernadotte, by Jewish terrorists, the Israeli Government forcibly disbanded the terrorists, and in February 1949 declared west Jerusalem an intregal part of Israel.

⊙ Jewish suburbs and villages captured by the Arabs during May and June 1948.

■ Jewish areas holding out against concerted Arab attacks from 15 May 1948, and completely cut off from the coast.

□ Arab suburbs and villages captured by Israeli forces, May to June 1948, and abandoned by their Arab inhabitants.

▬ ▬ Front line between the Israeli and Arab forces at the first cease-fire.

▨ Captured by Israeli forces between the first and second cease-fires.

▩ Captured by Israeli forces, October 1948.

● Arab villages occupied by Transjordan in 1948, and forming part of Jordan until 1967.

© Martin Gilbert 1977

Map 51

Plate 85   1 May 1948: during the Battle of Katamon, Jewish soldiers advance against an Arab fortified position in a private house.

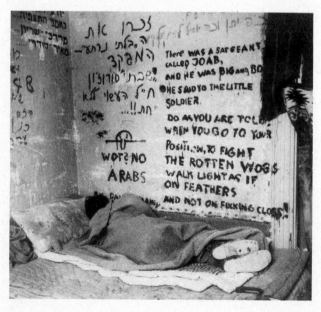

Plate 86   During a lull in the fighting in October 1948, an Israeli soldier sleeps, surrounded by British graffiti and a Hebrew notice: "Remember the Commander who never recoiled, Shabtai Sorotzon, a fearless soldier".

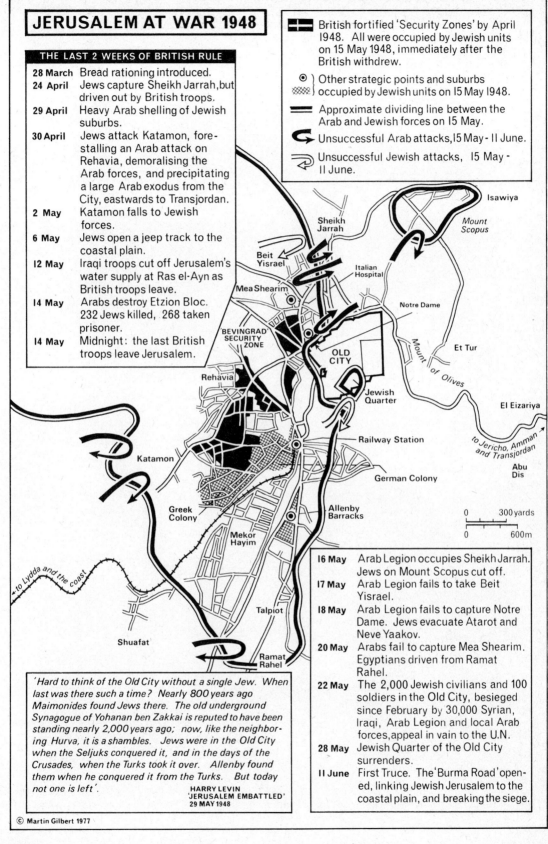

JERUSALEM AT WAR 1948

THE LAST 2 WEEKS OF BRITISH RULE

28 March	Bread rationing introduced.
24 April	Jews capture Sheikh Jarrah, but driven out by British troops.
29 April	Heavy Arab shelling of Jewish suburbs.
30 April	Jews attack Katamon, fore-stalling an Arab attack on Rehavia, demoralising the Arab forces, and precipitating a large Arab exodus from the City, eastwards to Transjordan.
2 May	Katamon falls to Jewish forces.
6 May	Jews open a jeep track to the coastal plain.
12 May	Iraqi troops cut off Jerusalem's water supply at Ras el-Ayn as British troops leave.
14 May	Arabs destroy Etzion Bloc. 232 Jews killed, 268 taken prisoner.
14 May	Midnight: the last British troops leave Jerusalem.

British fortified 'Security Zones' by April 1948. All were occupied by Jewish units on 15 May 1948, immediately after the British withdrew.

Other strategic points and suburbs occupied by Jewish units on 15 May 1948.

Approximate dividing line between the Arab and Jewish forces on 15 May.

Unsuccessful Arab attacks, 15 May - 11 June.

Unsuccessful Jewish attacks, 15 May - 11 June.

Map labels: Isawiya, Sheikh Jarrah, Mount Scopus, Beit Yisrael, Italian Hospital, Mea Shearim, Notre Dame, Et Tur, 'BEVINGRAD' SECURITY ZONE, OLD CITY, Rehavia, Jewish Quarter, El Eizariya, Katamon, Railway Station, to Jericho, Amman and Transjordan, Abu Dis, German Colony, Greek Colony, Allenby Barracks, Mekor Hayim, to Lydda and the coast, Talpiot, Shuafat, Ramat Rahel

0 300 yards
0 600m

16 May	Arab Legion occupies Sheikh Jarrah. Jews on Mount Scopus cut off.
17 May	Arab Legion fails to take Beit Yisrael.
18 May	Arab Legion fails to capture Notre Dame. Jews evacuate Atarot and Neve Yaakov.
20 May	Arabs fail to capture Mea Shearim. Egyptians driven from Ramat Rahel.
22 May	The 2,000 Jewish civilians and 100 soldiers in the Old City, besieged since February by 30,000 Syrian, Iraqi, Arab Legion and local Arab forces, appeal in vain to the U.N.
28 May	Jewish Quarter of the Old City surrenders.
11 June	First Truce. The 'Burma Road' opened, linking Jewish Jerusalem to the coastal plain, and breaking the siege.

'Hard to think of the Old City without a single Jew. When last was there such a time? Nearly 800 years ago Maimonides found Jews there. The old underground Synagogue of Yohanan ben Zakkai is reputed to have been standing nearly 2,000 years ago; now, like the neighboring Hurva, it is a shambles. Jews were in the Old City when the Seljuks conquered it, and in the days of the Crusades, when the Turks took it over. Allenby found them when he conquered it from the Turks. But today not one is left'.

HARRY LEVIN
'JERUSALEM EMBATTLED'
29 MAY 1948

© Martin Gilbert 1977

Map 52

97

Plate 87   The north-west corner of the Old City, outside the walls, looking towards the Jaffa Gate. A photograph taken from the Israeli sector in December 1948 overlooking 'No-Man's Land.

Plate 88   Arab Legion soldiers from Trans-Jordan (left), and Israeli Military Police, on guard at Government House, 24 January 1949, awaiting the arrival of the United Nations Conciliation Commission.

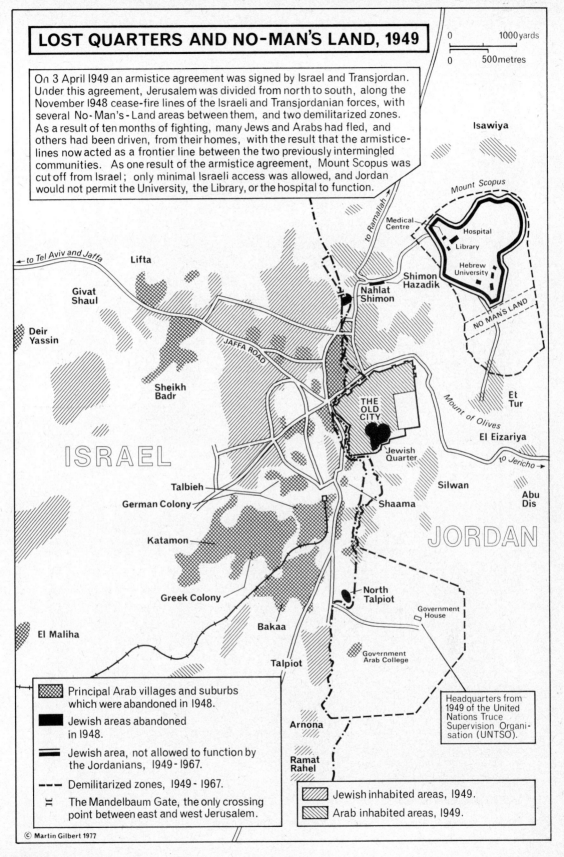

LOST QUARTERS AND NO-MAN'S LAND, 1949

0 ____ 1000 yards

0 ____ 500 metres

On 3 April 1949 an armistice agreement was signed by Israel and Transjordan. Under this agreement, Jerusalem was divided from north to south, along the November 1948 cease-fire lines of the Israeli and Transjordanian forces, with several No-Man's-Land areas between them, and two demilitarized zones. As a result of ten months of fighting, many Jews and Arabs had fled, and others had been driven, from their homes, with the result that the armistice-lines now acted as a frontier line between the two previously intermingled communities. As one result of the armistice agreement, Mount Scopus was cut off from Israel; only minimal Israeli access was allowed, and Jordan would not permit the University, the Library, or the hospital to function.

Isawiya

Mount Scopus

Medical Centre

Hospital

Library

Hebrew University

NO MAN'S LAND

← to Tel Aviv and Jaffa

Lifta

Givat Shaul

Deir Yassin

Shimon Hazadik

Nahlat Shimon

to Ramallah

JAFFA ROAD

Sheikh Badr

Et Tur

THE OLD CITY

Mount of Olives

ISRAEL

Jewish Quarter

El Eizariya

to Jericho →

Talbieh

German Colony

Silwan

Abu Dis

Shaama

Katamon

JORDAN

Greek Colony

North Talpiot

Government House

Bakaa

El Maliha

Government Arab College

Talpiot

Principal Arab villages and suburbs which were abandoned in 1948.

Jewish areas abandoned in 1948.

Jewish area, not allowed to function by the Jordanians, 1949-1967.

Demilitarized zones, 1949-1967.

The Mandelbaum Gate, the only crossing point between east and west Jerusalem.

Arnona

Ramat Rahel

Headquarters from 1949 of the United Nations Truce Supervision Organisation (UNTSO).

Jewish inhabited areas, 1949.

Arab inhabited areas, 1949.

© Martin Gilbert 1977

Map 53

Plate 89 A "sniper's wall" in the Jaffa road, near the north-west corner of the Old City, built to protect the citizens of Israel's capital from sniper fire from Jordanian troops on the City Wall.

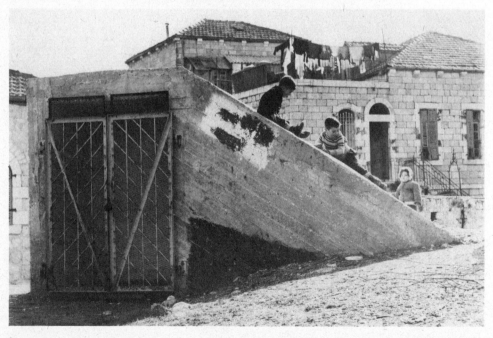

Plate 90 A shelter in the Israeli suburb of Musrara, near the armistice line; a photograph taken in 1966.

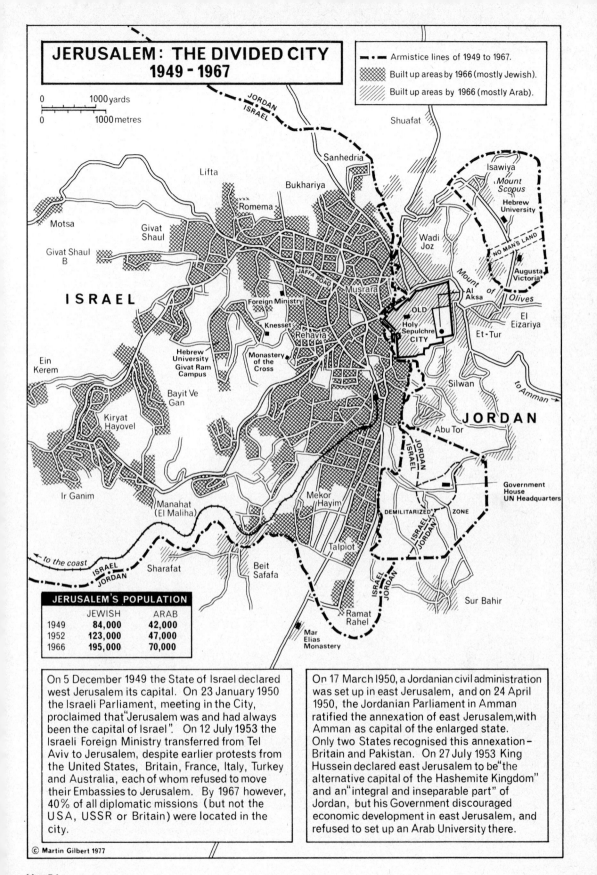

JERUSALEM: THE DIVIDED CITY 1949-1967

- ━·━ Armistice lines of 1949 to 1967.
- ▨ Built up areas by 1966 (mostly Jewish).
- ▨ Built up areas by 1966 (mostly Arab).

0 1000 yards
0 1000 metres

JORDAN ISRAEL

Shuafat

Sanhedria

Lifta

Bukhariya

Romema

Isawiya
Mount Scopus
Hebrew University

Motsa

Givat Shaul

Givat Shaul B

Wadi Joz

NO MAN'S LAND

Augusta Victoria

ISRAEL

JAFFA ROAD

Musrara

Mount of Olives

Foreign Ministry

OLD CITY

Al Aksa

Knesset

Holy Sepulchre

El Eizariya

Rehavia

Et-Tur

Ein Kerem

Hebrew University Givat Ram Campus

Monastery of the Cross

Silwan

Bayit Ve Gan

to Amman

JORDAN

Kiryat Hayovel

Abu Tor

JORDAN ISRAEL

Ir Ganim

Government House UN Headquarters

Manahat (El Maliha)

Mekor Hayim

DEMILITARIZED ZONE

ISRAEL JORDAN

Talpiot

to the coast

ISRAEL JORDAN

Sharafat

Beit Safafa

ISRAEL JORDAN

Sur Bahir

Ramat Rahel

Mar Elias Monastery

JERUSALEM'S POPULATION

	JEWISH	ARAB
1949	84,000	42,000
1952	123,000	47,000
1966	195,000	70,000

On 5 December 1949 the State of Israel declared west Jerusalem its capital. On 23 January 1950 the Israeli Parliament, meeting in the City, proclaimed that "Jerusalem was and had always been the capital of Israel". On 12 July 1953 the Israeli Foreign Ministry transferred from Tel Aviv to Jerusalem, despite earlier protests from the United States, Britain, France, Italy, Turkey and Australia, each of whom refused to move their Embassies to Jerusalem. By 1967 however, 40% of all diplomatic missions (but not the USA, USSR or Britain) were located in the city.

On 17 March 1950, a Jordanian civil administration was set up in east Jerusalem, and on 24 April 1950, the Jordanian Parliament in Amman ratified the annexation of east Jerusalem, with Amman as capital of the enlarged state. Only two States recognised this annexation – Britain and Pakistan. On 27 July 1953 King Hussein declared east Jerusalem to be "the alternative capital of the Hashemite Kingdom" and an "integral and inseparable part" of Jordan, but his Government discouraged economic development in east Jerusalem, and refused to set up an Arab University there.

© Martin Gilbert 1977

Map 54

Plate 91 The interior of the 'Middle' Synagogue in the Old City, in continuous use by Jewish worshippers from the eighteenth century to 1948, when it was gutted during the fighting. During the Jordanian rule the synagogue was used as a sheep and goat pen, Jews being denied access to it. This photograph was taken on 29 June 1967, immediately after the reunification of the City under Israeli rule.

Plate 92 Tombstones from the desecrated Jewish cemetery on the Mount of Olives used as stepping stones to a lavatory in a Jordanian Army Camp on the Jericho road; a photograph taken shortly after the reunification of the City in June 1967.

DIVIDED JERUSALEM AND THE HOLY PLACES, 1949-1967

Under Article VIII of the Israel-Jordan Armistice Agreement of 3 April 1949, Israeli Jews were guaranteed free access to the Western (or Wailing) Wall, but not to the Mount of Olives cemetery, the Kidron valley tombs, or the tomb of Simon the Just. In fact, no Israeli Jews were allowed to visit even the Western Wall during the nineteen years of Jordanian rule, a motor road was built through the Mount of Olives cemetery, tombstones were used as building materials, the Tomb of Simon the Just used as a stable, and the Synagogues of the Old City were demolished or desecrated.

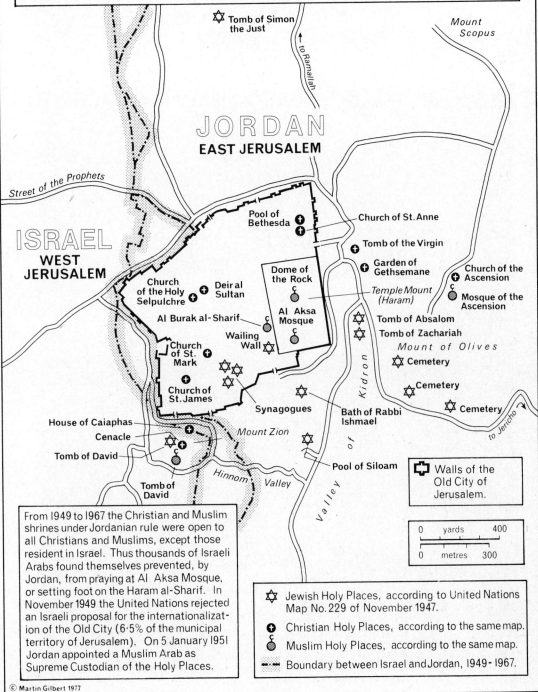

Tomb of Simon the Just

Mount Scopus

to Ramallah

JORDAN
EAST JERUSALEM

Street of the Prophets

ISRAEL
WEST JERUSALEM

Pool of Bethesda

Church of St. Anne

Tomb of the Virgin

Garden of Gethsemane

Church of the Ascension

Mosque of the Ascension

Church of the Holy Selpulchre

Deir al Sultan

Dome of the Rock

Temple Mount (Haram)

Al Burak al-Sharif

Al Aksa Mosque

Tomb of Absalom
Tomb of Zachariah

Mount of Olives

Wailing Wall

Church of St. Mark

Cemetery

Church of St. James

Synagogues

Bath of Rabbi Ishmael

Cemetery

Cemetery

House of Caiaphas

Cenacle

Tomb of David

Mount Zion

to Jericho

Tomb of David

Hinnom Valley

Pool of Siloam

Kidron

Valley of

Walls of the Old City of Jerusalem.

| 0 | yards | 400 |
| 0 | metres | 300 |

From 1949 to 1967 the Christian and Muslim shrines under Jordanian rule were open to all Christians and Muslims, except those resident in Israel. Thus thousands of Israeli Arabs found themselves prevented, by Jordan, from praying at Al Aksa Mosque, or setting foot on the Haram al-Sharif. In November 1949 the United Nations rejected an Israeli proposal for the internationalization of the Old City (6·5% of the municipal territory of Jerusalem). On 5 January 1951 Jordan appointed a Muslim Arab as Supreme Custodian of the Holy Places.

✡ Jewish Holy Places, according to United Nations Map No. 229 of November 1947.

✚ Christian Holy Places, according to the same map.

◗ Muslim Holy Places, according to the same map.

▬▬▬ Boundary between Israel and Jordan, 1949-1967.

© Martin Gilbert 1977

Map 55

103

Plate 93   The laundry at Ramat Rahel, destroyed during Egyptian and Arab Legion attacks in May 1948. This photograph was taken six months later.

Plate 94   The trench linking Ramat Rahel with Talpiot, October 1948.

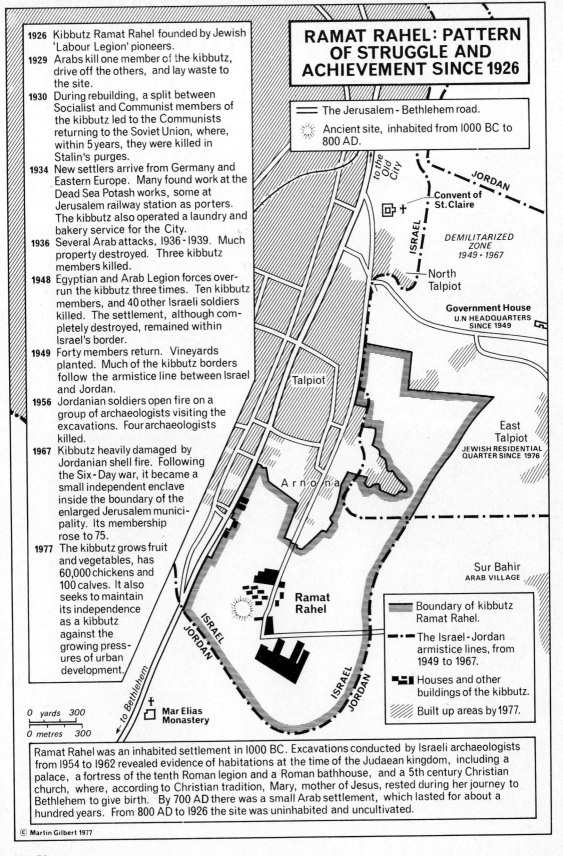

RAMAT RAHEL: PATTERN OF STRUGGLE AND ACHIEVEMENT SINCE 1926

1926 Kibbutz Ramat Rahel founded by Jewish 'Labour Legion' pioneers.

1929 Arabs kill one member of the kibbutz, drive off the others, and lay waste to the site.

1930 During rebuilding, a split between Socialist and Communist members of the kibbutz led to the Communists returning to the Soviet Union, where, within 5 years, they were killed in Stalin's purges.

1934 New settlers arrive from Germany and Eastern Europe. Many found work at the Dead Sea Potash works, some at Jerusalem railway station as porters. The kibbutz also operated a laundry and bakery service for the City.

1936 Several Arab attacks, 1936-1939. Much property destroyed. Three kibbutz members killed.

1948 Egyptian and Arab Legion forces over-run the kibbutz three times. Ten kibbutz members, and 40 other Israeli soldiers killed. The settlement, although completely destroyed, remained within Israel's border.

1949 Forty members return. Vineyards planted. Much of the kibbutz borders follow the armistice line between Israel and Jordan.

1956 Jordanian soldiers open fire on a group of archaeologists visiting the excavations. Four archaeologists killed.

1967 Kibbutz heavily damaged by Jordanian shell fire. Following the Six-Day war, it became a small independent enclave inside the boundary of the enlarged Jerusalem municipality. Its membership rose to 75.

1977 The kibbutz grows fruit and vegetables, has 60,000 chickens and 100 calves. It also seeks to maintain its independence as a kibbutz against the growing pressures of urban development.

The Jerusalem - Bethlehem road.

Ancient site, inhabited from 1000 BC to 800 AD.

to the Old City

JORDAN

ISRAEL

Convent of St. Claire

DEMILITARIZED ZONE 1949 - 1967

North Talpiot

Government House
U.N HEADQUARTERS SINCE 1949

Talpiot

East Talpiot
JEWISH RESIDENTIAL QUARTER SINCE 1976

Arnona

Sur Bahir
ARAB VILLAGE

Ramat Rahel

ISRAEL
JORDAN

ISRAEL
JORDAN

to Bethlehem

Mar Elias Monastery

0 yards 300

0 metres 300

Boundary of kibbutz Ramat Rahel.

The Israel - Jordan armistice lines, from 1949 to 1967.

Houses and other buildings of the kibbutz.

Built up areas by 1977.

Ramat Rahel was an inhabited settlement in 1000 BC. Excavations conducted by Israeli archaeologists from 1954 to 1962 revealed evidence of habitations at the time of the Judaean kingdom, including a palace, a fortress of the tenth Roman legion and a Roman bathhouse, and a 5th century Christian church, where, according to Christian tradition, Mary, mother of Jesus, rested during her journey to Bethlehem to give birth. By 700 AD there was a small Arab settlement, which lasted for about a hundred years. From 800 AD to 1926 the site was uninhabited and uncultivated.

© Martin Gilbert 1977

Map 56

105

Plate 95   As the Six-Day-War ends, two Orthodox Jews reach the desecrated Jewish Cemetery on the Mount of Olives. Behind them, the Haram enclosure, the Al Aksa Mosque (left) and the Dome of the Rock.

Plate 96   23 June 1967. The scene outside the Al Aksa mosque, after the first Friday prayer meeting since 1948 at which Arabs from the Israeli side of the Armistice line could be present. The Jordanians had for nineteen years refused to allow Israeli Arabs, as well as Israeli Jews, entry into east Jerusalem.

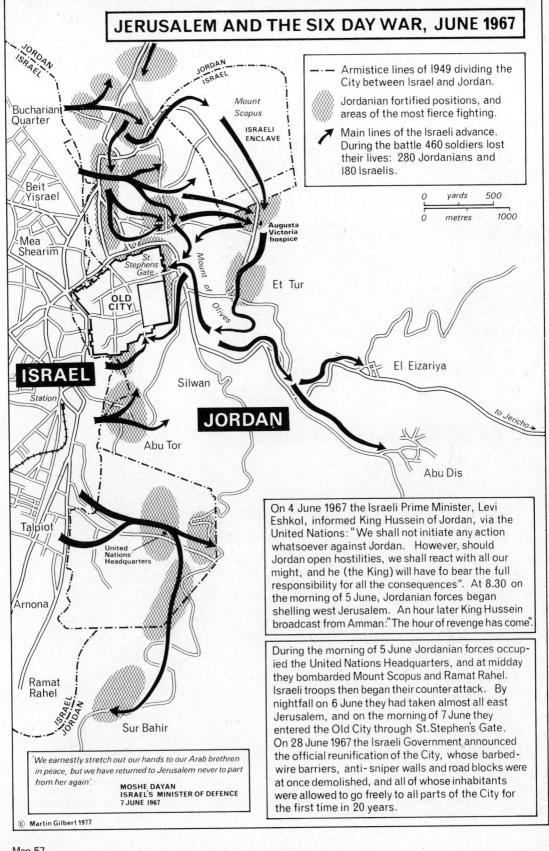

JERUSALEM AND THE SIX DAY WAR, JUNE 1967

— · — Armistice lines of 1949 dividing the City between Israel and Jordan.

Jordanian fortified positions, and areas of the most fierce fighting.

Main lines of the Israeli advance. During the battle 460 soldiers lost their lives: 280 Jordanians and 180 Israelis.

JORDAN
ISRAEL

Bucharian Quarter

JORDAN
ISRAEL

Mount Scopus

ISRAELI ENCLAVE

Beit Yisrael

Augusta Victoria hospice

Mea Shearim

St. Stephens Gate

Mount of Olives

Et Tur

OLD CITY

ISRAEL

Station

Silwan

JORDAN

El Eizariya

to Jericho

Abu Tor

Abu Dis

Talpiot

United Nations Headquarters

Arnona

0   yards   500
0   metres   1000

Ramat Rahel

ISRAEL
JORDAN

Sur Bahir

On 4 June 1967 the Israeli Prime Minister, Levi Eshkol, informed King Hussein of Jordan, via the United Nations: "We shall not initiate any action whatsoever against Jordan. However, should Jordan open hostilities, we shall react with all our might, and he (the King) will have to bear the full responsibility for all the consequences". At 8.30 on the morning of 5 June, Jordanian forces began shelling west Jerusalem. An hour later King Hussein broadcast from Amman: "The hour of revenge has come".

During the morning of 5 June Jordanian forces occupied the United Nations Headquarters, and at midday they bombarded Mount Scopus and Ramat Rahel. Israeli troops then began their counter attack. By nightfall on 6 June they had taken almost all east Jerusalem, and on the morning of 7 June they entered the Old City through St.Stephen's Gate. On 28 June 1967 the Israeli Government announced the official reunification of the City, whose barbed-wire barriers, anti-sniper walls and road blocks were at once demolished, and all of whose inhabitants were allowed to go freely to all parts of the City for the first time in 20 years.

'We earnestly stretch out our hands to our Arab brethren in peace, but we have returned to Jerusalem never to part from her again'.
MOSHE DAYAN
ISRAEL'S MINISTER OF DEFENCE
7 JUNE 1967

© Martin Gilbert 1977

Map 57

107

Plate 97 1951: Jordanian shells strike the Fast Hotel, just inside the Israeli side of the 1949 armistice line. Such shelling was never condemned by the United Nations, even when it resulted in destruction of property, injury, or loss of life. Nor did the United Nations condemn any of the Arab terrorist attacks in Jerusalem after 1967, when bombs were left in cars, streets, supermarkets and cafes, killing two students on 21 February 1969, fifteen passers-by (including three Arab women) on 4 July 1975, and seven teenagers on 13 November 1975.

Plate 98 Ramat Eshkol, one of the new Israeli suburbs built after 1967, east of the 1949 armistice line. On the hill behind Ramat Eshkol is the Arab village of Shuafat. On the hill to the right is another new Israeli suburb, Givat Hamivtar, in the process of construction. The United Nations has repeatedly condemned all Israeli housing projects east of the 1949 armistice lines.

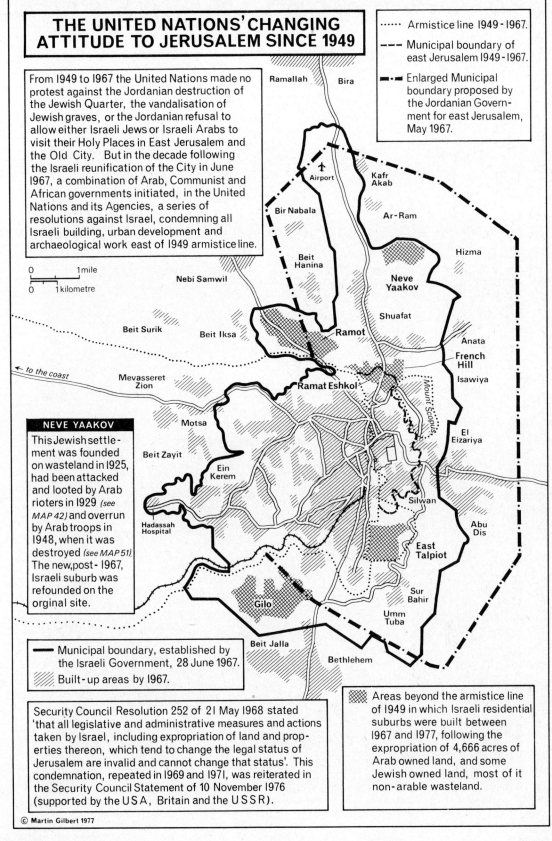

THE UNITED NATIONS' CHANGING ATTITUDE TO JERUSALEM SINCE 1949

.... Armistice line 1949-1967.

----- Municipal boundary of east Jerusalem 1949-1967.

-·-·- Enlarged Municipal boundary proposed by the Jordanian Government for east Jerusalem, May 1967.

From 1949 to 1967 the United Nations made no protest against the Jordanian destruction of the Jewish Quarter, the vandalisation of Jewish graves, or the Jordanian refusal to allow either Israeli Jews or Israeli Arabs to visit their Holy Places in East Jerusalem and the Old City. But in the decade following the Israeli reunification of the City in June 1967, a combination of Arab, Communist and African governments initiated, in the United Nations and its Agencies, a series of resolutions against Israel, condemning all Israeli building, urban development and archaeological work east of 1949 armistice line.

0   1 mile
0   1 kilometre

NEVE YAAKOV
This Jewish settle-
ment was founded
on wasteland in 1925,
had been attacked
and looted by Arab
rioters in 1929 (see
MAP 42) and overrun
by Arab troops in
1948, when it was
destroyed (see MAP 51).
The new, post- 1967,
Israeli suburb was
refounded on the
orginal site.

Ramallah   Bira
Airport
Kafr Akab
Bir Nabala
Ar-Ram
Hizma
Beit Hanina
Neve Yaakov
Nebi Samwil
Shuafat
Beit Surik   Beit Iksa
Ramot
Anata
French Hill
← to the coast
Mevasseret Zion
Ramat Eshkol
Isawiya
Mount Scopus
Motsa
El Eizariya
Beit Zayit
Ein Kerem
Silwan
Abu Dis
Hadassah Hospital
East Talpiot
Sur Bahir
Gilo
Umm Tuba
Beit Jalla   Bethlehem

——— Municipal boundary, established by the Israeli Government, 28 June 1967.

▨ Built-up areas by 1967.

Security Council Resolution 252 of 21 May 1968 stated 'that all legislative and administrative measures and actions taken by Israel, including expropriation of land and prop-erties thereon, which tend to change the legal status of Jerusalem are invalid and cannot change that status'. This condemnation, repeated in 1969 and 1971, was reiterated in the Security Council Statement of 10 November 1976 (supported by the USA, Britain and the USSR).

▨ Areas beyond the armistice line of 1949 in which Israeli residential suburbs were built between 1967 and 1977, following the expropriation of 4,666 acres of Arab owned land, and some Jewish owned land, most of it non-arable wasteland.

© Martin Gilbert 1977

Map 58

Plate 99   A project of the Jerusalem Foundation: laying water pipes in the bazaars of the Old City. A photograph taken on 26 August 1976.

Plate 100 Suq Khan Ez-Zeit (Bet Habad Street), in the Old City, one of several main bazaar streets in which the Jerusalem Foundation financed drainage and water works.

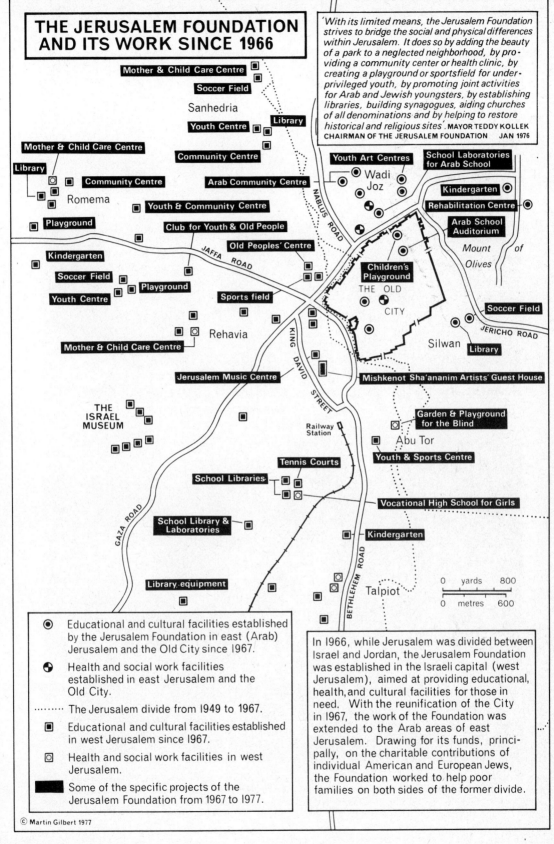

THE JERUSALEM FOUNDATION AND ITS WORK SINCE 1966

'With its limited means, the Jerusalem Foundation strives to bridge the social and physical differences within Jerusalem. It does so by adding the beauty of a park to a neglected neighborhood, by providing a community center or health clinic, by creating a playground or sportsfield for under-privileged youth, by promoting joint activities for Arab and Jewish youngsters, by establishing libraries, building synagogues, aiding churches of all denominations and by helping to restore historical and religious sites'. MAYOR TEDDY KOLLEK
CHAIRMAN OF THE JERUSALEM FOUNDATION   JAN 1976

Mother & Child Care Centre

Soccer Field

Sanhedria

Youth Centre   Library

Mother & Child Care Centre

Library

Community Centre

Community Centre

Romema

Arab Community Centre

Youth Art Centres   School Laboratories for Arab School

Wadi Joz

Kindergarten

Rehabilitation Centre

Arab School Auditorium

Mount   of

Olives

Youth & Community Centre

Playground

Club for Youth & Old People

Old Peoples' Centre

Children's Playground

THE OLD CITY

JAFFA ROAD

NABLUS ROAD

Kindergarten

Soccer Field

Youth Centre   Playground

Sports field

Soccer Field

JERICHO ROAD

Rehavia

Silwan   Library

KING DAVID STREET

Mother & Child Care Centre

Jerusalem Music Centre

Mishkenot Sha'ananim Artists' Guest House

THE ISRAEL MUSEUM

Railway Station

Garden & Playground for the Blind

Abu Tor

Youth & Sports Centre

Tennis Courts

School Libraries

Vocational High School for Girls

GAZA ROAD

School Library & Laboratories

Kindergarten

BETHLEHEM ROAD

Library equipment

Talpiot

0	yards	800
0	metres	600

⊙ Educational and cultural facilities established by the Jerusalem Foundation in east (Arab) Jerusalem and the Old City since 1967.

☥ Health and social work facilities established in east Jerusalem and the Old City.

········ The Jerusalem divide from 1949 to 1967.

▣ Educational and cultural facilities established in west Jerusalem since 1967.

▢ Health and social work facilities in west Jerusalem.

▬ Some of the specific projects of the Jerusalem Foundation from 1967 to 1977.

In 1966, while Jerusalem was divided between Israel and Jordan, the Jerusalem Foundation was established in the Israeli capital (west Jerusalem), aimed at providing educational, health, and cultural facilities for those in need. With the reunification of the City in 1967, the work of the Foundation was extended to the Arab areas of east Jerusalem. Drawing for its funds, principally, on the charitable contributions of individual American and European Jews, the Foundation worked to help poor families on both sides of the former divide.

© Martin Gilbert 1977

Map 59

111

Plate 101 The Sacher Park, 1961: moving stones and preparing the ground for planting.

Plate 102 The Sacher Park, 1964: as trees and shrubs begin to grow, Israeli families, Jewish immigrants from North Africa and Morocco, relax in the Park during the annual festival of Maimona, a time of picnics and merrymaking. Also, each year since 1967, Arab and Jewish children gather in the Park for an inter-communal youth festival, and for a municipal youth parliament.

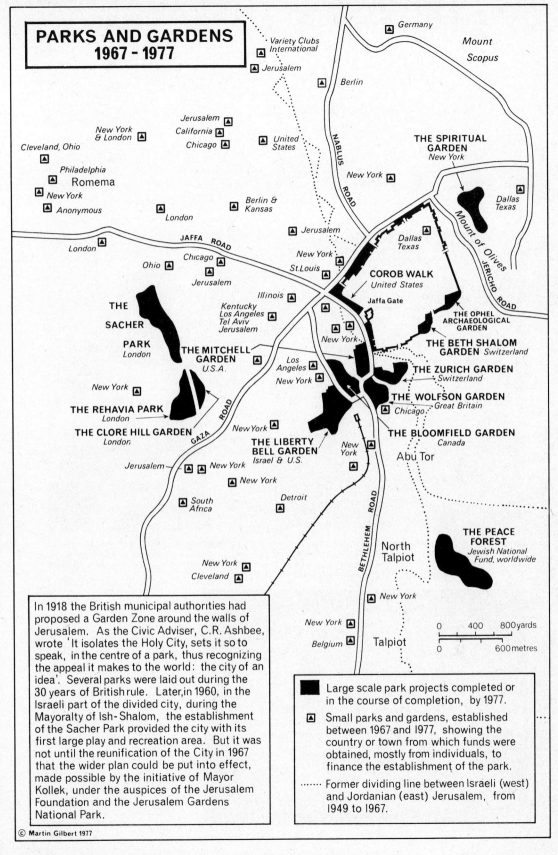

PARKS AND GARDENS
1967 - 1977

Germany

Mount Scopus

Variety Clubs International

Jerusalem

Berlin

NABLUS ROAD

THE SPIRITUAL GARDEN
New York

New York & London

Jerusalem
California
Chicago

United States

New York

Dallas Texas

Cleveland, Ohio

Philadelphia

Romema

New York

Anonymous

Berlin & Kansas

London

Jerusalem

Dallas Texas

Mount of Olives

JERICHO ROAD

London

JAFFA ROAD

Chicago

Ohio

St.Louis

Jerusalem

New York

COROB WALK
United States

Jaffa Gate

THE OPHEL ARCHAEOLOGICAL GARDEN

THE SACHER

Illinois

Kentucky
Los Angeles
Tel Aviv
Jerusalem

New York

THE BETH SHALOM GARDEN Switzerland

THE MITCHELL GARDEN
U.S.A.

PARK
London

THE ZURICH GARDEN
Switzerland

New York

Los Angeles

New York

THE WOLFSON GARDEN
Great Britain

THE REHAVIA PARK
London

GAZA ROAD

Chicago

THE CLORE HILL GARDEN
London

New York

THE BLOOMFIELD GARDEN
Canada

Jerusalem

New York

THE LIBERTY BELL GARDEN
Israel & U.S.

New York

Abu Tor

New York

South Africa

Detroit

BETHLEHEM ROAD

North Talpiot

THE PEACE FOREST
Jewish National Fund, worldwide

New York
Cleveland

New York

New York

Talpiot

0   400   800 yards

0   600 metres

In 1918 the British municipal authorities had proposed a Garden Zone around the walls of Jerusalem. As the Civic Adviser, C.R. Ashbee, wrote 'It isolates the Holy City, sets it so to speak, in the centre of a park, thus recognizing the appeal it makes to the world: the city of an idea'. Several parks were laid out during the 30 years of British rule. Later, in 1960, in the Israeli part of the divided city, during the Mayoralty of Ish-Shalom, the establishment of the Sacher Park provided the city with its first large play and recreation area. But it was not until the reunification of the City in 1967 that the wider plan could be put into effect, made possible by the initiative of Mayor Kollek, under the auspices of the Jerusalem Foundation and the Jerusalem Gardens National Park.

■ Large scale park projects completed or in the course of completion, by 1977.

▲ Small parks and gardens, established between 1967 and 1977, showing the country or town from which funds were obtained, mostly from individuals, to finance the establishment of the park.

⋯⋯ Former dividing line between Israeli (west) and Jordanian (east) Jerusalem, from 1949 to 1967.

Belgium

Map 60

113

Plate 103 A large Herodian house revealed on the western hill, during the Jewish Quarter excavations of 1974. Upper centre, the dome of the Al Aksa Mosque. During excavations at the base of the Old City Wall, the Israeli archaeologist Benjamin Mazar uncovered previously unrecorded early Muslim buildings of the Ommayad period (from 637 AD).

Plate 104 An ornamental architectural fragment of the Herodian period, found among debris at the Southern Wall.

ARCHAEOLOGICAL EXPLORATIONS SINCE 1914

The Ottoman, British, Jordanian and Israeli authorities each in turn permitted archaeological work in Jerusalem, with the result that a comprehensive picture now exists of the City's development from ancient times. Since 1925 the Department of Antiquities at the Hebrew University played a major part in many excavations, but between 1949 to 1967 the Jordanians refused to allow any Israeli archaeologists to excavate Jewish sites in east Jerusalem.

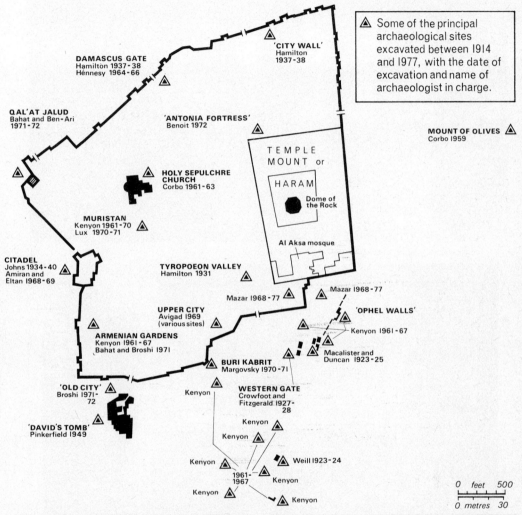

'THIRD WALL'
Sukenik and Mayer 1925-27
Ben-Arieh and Netzer 1972-73

▲ Some of the principal archaeological sites excavated between 1914 and 1977, with the date of excavation and name of archaeologist in charge.

'CITY WALL'
Hamilton 1937-38

DAMASCUS GATE
Hamilton 1937-38
Hennesy 1964-66

Q AL'AT JALUD
Bahat and Ben-Ari 1971-72

'ANTONIA FORTRESS'
Benoit 1972

MOUNT OF OLIVES ▲
Corbo 1959

TEMPLE MOUNT or
HARAM
Dome of the Rock
Al Aksa mosque

HOLY SEPULCHRE CHURCH
Corbo 1961-63

MURISTAN
Kenyon 1961-70
Lux 1970-71

CITADEL
Johns 1934-40
Amiran and Eltan 1968-69

TYROPOEON VALLEY
Hamilton 1931

Mazar 1968-77

Mazar 1968-77

'OPHEL WALLS'

UPPER CITY
Avigad 1969
(various sites)

Kenyon 1961-67

ARMENIAN GARDENS
Kenyon 1961-67
Bahat and Broshi 1971

Macalister and Duncan 1923-25

BURI KABRIT
Margovsky 1970-71

'OLD CITY'
Broshi 1971-72

Kenyon

WESTERN GATE
Crowfoot and Fitzgerald 1927-28

'DAVID'S TOMB'
Pinkerfield 1949

Kenyon

Kenyon

Kenyon

Weill 1923-24

1961-1967

Kenyon

Kenyon

Kenyon

0 feet 500
0 metres 30

On 7 November 1974 a United Nations Agency, UNESCO, condemned the Government of Israel for 'altering the cultural and historical character' of Jerusalem, in regard especially to Muslim and Christian sites, by the excavations undertaken since 1967. An independent inquiry, however, itself sponsored by UNESCO, had, on 17 May 1974, stressed both the professional care, and also the positive results to all three faiths, of Israel's archaeological efforts.

'The excavations are being carried out by a perfectly well qualified team of experts of various kinds, who are extremely attentive to all aspects and to all the periods of which remains have been found on the site. The same care is expended on the preservation of remains of the Ommiad palaces as on those of the Herodian period'.

BELGIAN PROFESSOR RAYMOND LEMAIRE, REPORT TO UNESCO, 1974

© Martin Gilbert 1977

Map 61

115

Plate 105 Jerusalemites queueing for water during the siege.

Plate 106 Emergency water supplies during the siege.

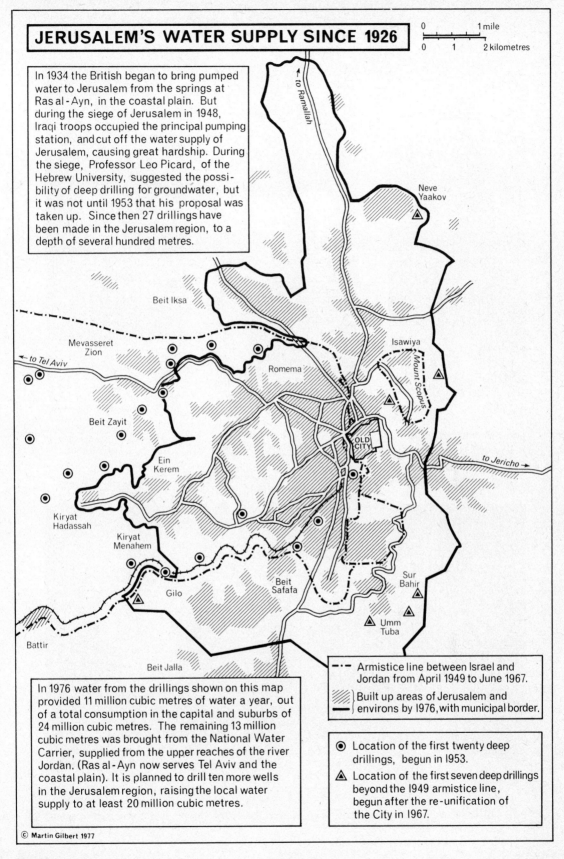

JERUSALEM'S WATER SUPPLY SINCE 1926

0 ___ 1 mile
0 ___ 1 ___ 2 kilometres

In 1934 the British began to bring pumped water to Jerusalem from the springs at Ras al - Ayn, in the coastal plain. But during the siege of Jerusalem in 1948, Iraqi troops occupied the principal pumping station, and cut off the water supply of Jerusalem, causing great hardship. During the siege, Professor Leo Picard, of the Hebrew University, suggested the possibility of deep drilling for groundwater, but it was not until 1953 that his proposal was taken up. Since then 27 drillings have been made in the Jerusalem region, to a depth of several hundred metres.

to Ramallah

Neve Yaakov

Beit Iksa

Mevasseret Zion

← to Tel Aviv

Romema

Isawiya

Mount Scopus

Beit Zayit

OLD CITY

to Jericho →

Ein Kerem

Kiryat Hadassah

Kiryat Menahem

Sur Bahir

Gilo

Beit Safafa

Umm Tuba

Battir

Beit Jalla

In 1976 water from the drillings shown on this map provided 11 million cubic metres of water a year, out of a total consumption in the capital and suburbs of 24 million cubic metres. The remaining 13 million cubic metres was brought from the National Water Carrier, supplied from the upper reaches of the river Jordan. (Ras al - Ayn now serves Tel Aviv and the coastal plain). It is planned to drill ten more wells in the Jerusalem region, raising the local water supply to at least 20 million cubic metres.

-·-·- Armistice line between Israel and Jordan from April 1949 to June 1967.

///// Built up areas of Jerusalem and environs by 1976, with municipal border.

⊙ Location of the first twenty deep drillings, begun in 1953.

△ Location of the first seven deep drillings beyond the 1949 armistice line, begun after the re-unification of the City in 1967.

© Martin Gilbert 1977

Map 62

Plate 109 King Hussein of Jordan, aged 17, on his first visit to Jerusalem as King, following the assassination in July 1951 of his grandfather, King Abdullah by an Arab gunman at the Al Aksa Mosque.

Plate 107 Jerusalem under Ottoman Rule: the Turkish Military Commander, Jamal Pasha; photographed in 1915

Plate 108 Jerusalem under British rule: the last British High Commissioner, General Sir Alan Cunningham, photographed in Government House in 1946.

Plate 110 The first Prime Minister of the State of Israel, David Ben Gurion, on his way to the opening session of the first Israeli Parliament to meet in Jerusalem, 14 February 1949.

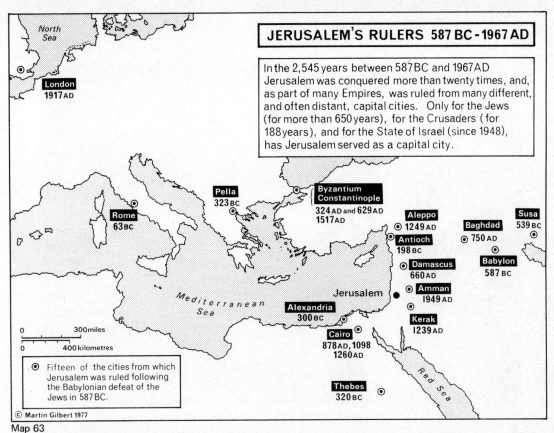

JERUSALEM'S RULERS 587 BC - 1967 AD

In the 2,545 years between 587 BC and 1967 AD Jerusalem was conquered more than twenty times, and, as part of many Empires, was ruled from many different, and often distant, capital cities. Only for the Jews (for more than 650 years), for the Crusaders (for 188 years), and for the State of Israel (since 1948), has Jerusalem served as a capital city.

London 1917 AD

North Sea

Rome 63 BC

Pella 323 BC

Byzantium Constantinople 324 AD and 629 AD 1517 AD

Aleppo 1249 AD

Baghdad 750 AD

Susa 539 BC

Antioch 198 BC

Damascus 660 AD

Babylon 587 BC

Jerusalem

Amman 1949 AD

Alexandria 300 BC

Kerak 1239 AD

Mediterranean Sea

Cairo 878 AD, 1098 1260 AD

Red Sea

Thebes 320 BC

0   300 miles
0   400 kilometres

⊙ Fifteen of the cities from which Jerusalem was ruled following the Babylonian defeat of the Jews in 587 BC.

© Martin Gilbert 1977

Map 63

JERUSALEM: CAPITAL OF THE STATE OF ISRAEL SINCE 1949

Western Jerusalem became the capital of the State of Israel in 1949. Reunited by Israel in 1967, the City was then freed from the problems and restrictions of a divided city, and became increasingly the focal point of Israeli cultural, social and political life.

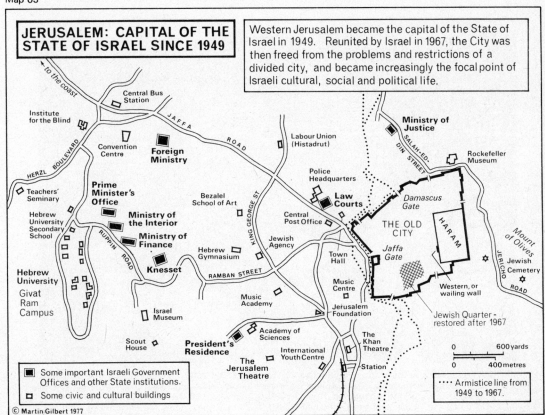

to the coast

Central Bus Station

Institute for the Blind

JAFFA ROAD

Ministry of Justice

Labour Union (Histadrut)

Rockefeller Museum

HERZL BOULEVARD

Convention Centre

Foreign Ministry

Police Headquarters

SALAH-ED-DIN STREET

Teachers' Seminary

Prime Minister's Office

Bezalel School of Art

Law Courts

Damascus Gate

Hebrew University Secondary School

Ministry of the Interior

Central Post Office

THE OLD CITY

HARAM

Mount of Olives

RUPPIN ROAD

Ministry of Finance

Hebrew Gymnasium

Jewish Agency

Town Hall

Jaffa Gate

JERICHO ROAD

Jewish Cemetery

Hebrew University Givat Ram Campus

Knesset

KING GEORGE ST

RAMBAN STREET

Western, or wailing wall

Music Centre

Music Academy

Israel Museum

Jerusalem Foundation

Jewish Quarter - restored after 1967

Scout House

President's Residence

Academy of Sciences

The Khan Theatre

International Youth Centre

The Jerusalem Theatre

Station

0   600 yards
0   400 metres

■ Some important Israeli Government Offices and other State institutions.

□ Some civic and cultural buildings

···· Armistice line from 1949 to 1967.

© Martin Gilbert 1977

Map 64

Plate 111 The YMCA (left, with tower, cupola and tennis court) built in 1933, and the King David Hotel (right) built in 1930, with British flags; a photograph taken in 1937 at the time of the coronation of King George VI.

Plate 112 Temporary housing for new immigrants, Talpiot, 1950. Jews immigrating from Arab lands - including Morocco, Libya, Iraq and the Yemen — played an important part in the increase in Jerusalem's Jewish population from 69,000 in 1949 to 166,000 by 1961. By 1965 most of these immigrants had been rehoused in new apartments, and the temporary housing replaced by modern buildings.

1845

1910

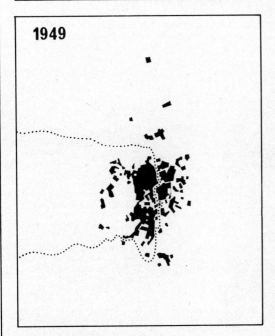

1949

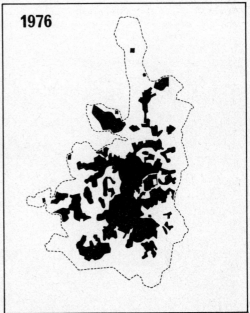

1976

■ Built-up areas of Jerusalem, in 1845, 1910, 1949 and 1976.

······· Armistice line of 1949 to 1967 (1949 map only).

----- Municipal boundary established in 1967 (1976 map only).

In 1845 the Prussian Consul in Jerusalem, Dr Schultz, estimated the City's population as 7,120 Jews, 5,000 Muslim Arabs, and 3,390 Christian Arabs. By 1912 the population had grown to approximately 45,000 Jews and 35,000 Arabs. By 1976 it had risen to more than 260,000 Jews and 96,000 Arabs.

© Martin Gilbert 1977

Map 65

Plate 113 Jerusalem, 20 May, 1974: Teddy Kollek, Mayor of Jerusalem from 1966, speaks at a memorial ceremony for soldiers who lost their lives during one of the battles for Jerusalem seven years earlier.

Plate 114 Jerusalem, 12 October 1976. During the pilgrim festival of Succot (Tabernacles), Jews from all over Israel gather at the western, or 'wailing' wall of their ancient Temple Mount (see also Map 9). Since 1967 Jews from all over the world have come daily to pray at the wall. Behind the wall is the cupola of the Dome of the Rock, itself the scene of Muslim pilgrimage from all over the Islamic world. To the left is the Minaret of the Chain, built in 1329, ten years after the reconstruction of the Dome of the Rock. The building on the left, with the four large windows, belongs to the Muslim Religious Foundation (the WAKF), and was formerly the Muslim Religious Court.

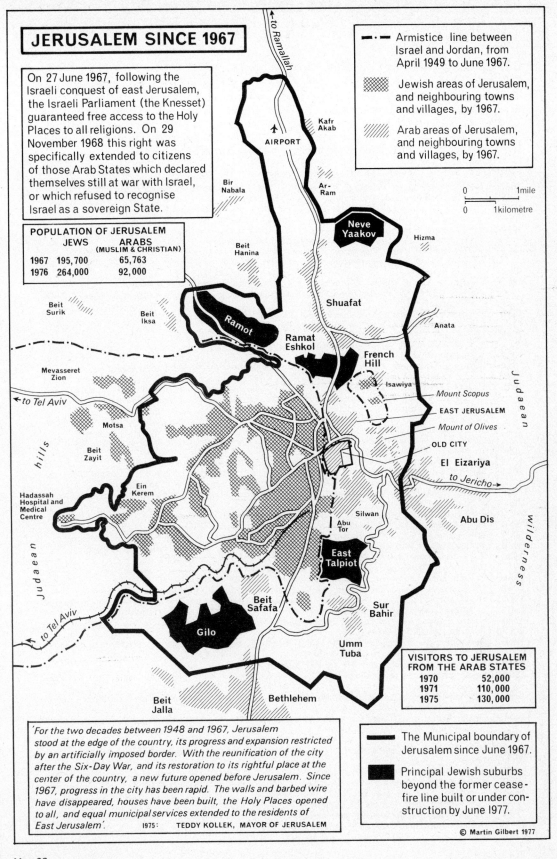

JERUSALEM SINCE 1967

On 27 June 1967, following the Israeli conquest of east Jerusalem, the Israeli Parliament (the Knesset) guaranteed free access to the Holy Places to all religions. On 29 November 1968 this right was specifically extended to citizens of those Arab States which declared themselves still at war with Israel, or which refused to recognise Israel as a sovereign State.

POPULATION OF JERUSALEM

	JEWS	ARABS (MUSLIM & CHRISTIAN)
1967	195,700	65,763
1976	264,000	92,000

- ·-··- Armistice line between Israel and Jordan, from April 1949 to June 1967.
- Jewish areas of Jerusalem, and neighbouring towns and villages, by 1967.
- Arab areas of Jerusalem, and neighbouring towns and villages, by 1967.

0   1mile
0   1kilometre

VISITORS TO JERUSALEM FROM THE ARAB STATES

1970	52,000
1971	110,000
1975	130,000

Map labels: to Ramallah, AIRPORT, Kafr Akab, Bir Nabala, Ar-Ram, Beit Hanina, Neve Yaakov, Hizma, Beit Surik, Beit Iksa, Ramot, Shuafat, Anata, Mevasseret Zion, Ramat Eshkol, French Hill, Isawiya, Mount Scopus, EAST JERUSALEM, Mount of Olives, to Tel Aviv, Motsa, OLD CITY, El Eizariya, to Jericho, Beit Zayit, Ein Kerem, Hadassah Hospital and Medical Centre, Silwan, Abu Dis, Judaean hills, Abu Tor, East Talpiot, Sur Bahir, Beit Safafa, Gilo, Umm Tuba, to Tel Aviv, Judaean wilderness, Beit Jalla, Bethlehem

'For the two decades between 1948 and 1967, Jerusalem stood at the edge of the country, its progress and expansion restricted by an artificially imposed border. With the reunification of the city after the Six-Day War, and its restoration to its rightful place at the center of the country, a new future opened before Jerusalem. Since 1967, progress in the city has been rapid. The walls and barbed wire have disappeared, houses have been built, the Holy Places opened to all, and equal municipal services extended to the residents of East Jerusalem'.   1975:   TEDDY KOLLEK, MAYOR OF JERUSALEM

- The Municipal boundary of Jerusalem since June 1967.
- Principal Jewish suburbs beyond the former cease-fire line built or under construction by June 1977.

© Martin Gilbert 1977

Map 66

123

Bibliography of Works Consulted

This bibliography is limited to those books which I have consulted for the preparation of this volume. Part One consists of Atlases, single sheet maps, and guide books, which I have listed in order of publication, year-by-year. Part Two consists of books written by pilgrims to the City, travellers, missionaries, tourists, soldiers, surveyors, and town planners, between 1615 and 1976, also listed in order of publication. Part Three consists of historical works, biographies and memoirs, listed in alphabetical order according to their authors.

PART ONE: Atlases, single sheet maps and guide books

1833   *Land of Moriah or Environs of Jerusalem,* published for the Proprietors of Scotts Bible by L.B. Sealey & Sons. Drawn and Engraved by Thos. Stanley (London)

1835   Dr. Ernst Gustav Schultz, *Plan von Jerusalem,* single sheet map, scale 1:6,000 (Bern)

1853   Titus Tobler, *Topographie von Jerusalem und Seinen Umgebungen* (Berlin)

1858   John Murray, *Handbook for Travellers in the Holy Land: Syria, Palestine, Moab etc.* (London)

        Titus Tobler, *Planography of Jerusalem* (Gotha and London)

        C.M.W. Van de Velde, *Plan of the Town and Environs of Jerusalem constructed from the English Ordnance-Survey and measurements of Dr. T. Tobler,* single sheet map, scale 1:4843 (Gotha and London)

1865   Captain Charles W. Wilson, *Ordnance Survey of Jerusalem,* 4 volumes (London)

        Captain Charles W. Wilson, *Plan of Jerusalem with Contours,* single sheet map, scale 1:2,500 (London)

1876   K. Baedeker (editor), *Palestine and Syria* (Leipzig)

        Cook's Tourists' Handbook for Palestine and Syria (London)

1901   Macmillan's *Guide to Palestine and Egypt* (London)

        E.A. Reynolds-Ball, *Jerusalem: A Practical Guide to Jerusalem and its Environs* (London)

1907   Father Barnabas Meistermann, *New Guide to the Holy Land* (London);

1915   George Adam Smith, *Atlas of the Historical Geography of the Holy Land* (London)

1917   Survey of Egypt, *Environs of Jerusalem,* single sheet map, scale 1:25,000 (Cairo)

1918   Palestine Pocket Guide-Books, *Volume 1: A Guide Book to Southern Palestine . . . Based upon the well-known enemy publication Baedeker's Palestine and Syria and augmented by numerous additions* (Cairo)

        Royal Engineers, Egyptian Expeditionary Force, *Jerusalem Water Supply,* single sheet map, scale 1:40,000 (Jerusalem)

        Royal Engineers, Egyptian Expeditionary Force, *Town Distribution System,* single sheet map, scale 1:20,000

        Survey of Egypt, *Jerusalem,* single sheet map, scale 1:11,000 (Cairo)

1921   J. Press, *Jerusalem und Nähere Umgebung,* single sheet map, scale 1:10,000 (Jerusalem)

        Jesaias Press, *Palästina und Sudsyrien Reisehandbuch* (Jerusalem, Berlin and Vienna)

1922   Henry Charles Luke and Edward Keith-Roach, *The Handbook of Palestine and Transjordan* (London)

        Professeurs de Notre-Dame de France à Jérusalem, *La Palestine* (Paris)

1924   Harry Charles Luke, *A Guide to Jerusalem and Judea* (London)

1929   E.F. Beaumont, *Plan of Jerusalem and Environs,* single sheet map, scale 1:8,000 (Jerusalem)

1930   G. Olaf Matson, *The American Coloney Palestine Guide,* 3rd extended edition (Jerusalem)

1935   Zev Vilnay, *Steimatzky's Guide: Jerusalem and Its Environs* (Jerusalem)

        Zev Vilnay, *Steimatzky's Palestine Guide* (Jerusalem)

1938   Z. Friedländer, *Jerusalem,* single sheet map, scale 1:7,500 (Haifa)

1942   Dr. Benjamin Maisler, *The Graphic Historical Atlas of Palestine* (Tel Aviv)

1946   His Majesty's Stationery Office, *Maps Relating to the Report of the Anglo-American Committee of Enquiry regarding the Problems of European Jewry and Palestine* (London)

1949   United Nations, *Central Portion of the Jerusalem Area: Principal Holy Places,* single sheet map, scale 1:10,000 (UN Map 229)

1952   Geographic Section, General Staff War Office (GSGS 8055) *Jerusalem Town Plan,* single sheet maps 1 to 6 scale 1:10,000 (London)

1956   Fr Eugene Hoade, *Jerusalem and Its Environs* (Jerusalem)

1963   Department of Surveys, Ministry of Labour, *Jerusalem,* single sheet map, scale 1:10,000 (Tel Aviv)

1965   Assali Showrooms, *Jerusalem: Jordan: The Holy Land,* single sheet map, scale 1:5,000 (Jerusalem, Jordan)

        Khalid Assaly, *Jerusalem (Jordan) and Region Planning Proposals, November 1964,* single sheet map, scale 1:25,000 (London)

PART TWO: Books by pilgrims to the City, travellers, missionaries, tourists, soldiers, surveyors and town planners

1615   George Sandys, *A Relation of a Journey Begun in An: Dom: 1610* (London)

1670   Michiel Miloco, *Viaggio da Venetia al Santo Sepolcro et al Monte Sinai* (Venice)

1684   *Hierusalem, or the Pilgrim and His Guide* (London)

1702   R.P. Michael Naud, *Voyage Nouveau de la Terre-Sainte* (Paris)

1703   Henry Maundrell, *A Journey from Aleppo to Jerusalem at Easter, A.D. 1696* (Oxford)

1719   Nath Crouch, *Two Journeys to Jerusalem* (London)

1766   Frederick Hasselquist, *Voyages and Travels in the Levant in the Years 1749, 50, 51,52* (London)
1787   Constantin Francois Chasseboeuf, Comte de Volney, *Travels Through Syria and Egypt* (London)
1811   F.A. de Chateaubriand, *Travels in Greece, Palestine, Egypt, and Barbary During the Years 1806 and 1807,* 2 volumes, translated by Frederic Shoberl (London)
1832   The Rev Michael Russell, *Palestine or the Holy Land* (Edinburgh and London)
1833   R.R. Madden, *Travels in Turkey, Egypt, Nubia and Palestine in 1824, 1825, 1826 & 1827,* 2 volumes (London)
1835   The Rev Thomas Hartwell Horne, *Landscape Illustrations of the Bible,* 2 volumes (London)
        Jewish Intelligence and Monthly Account of the Proceedings of the London Society for Promoting Christianity Among the Jews, 26 volumes (London, 1835-1860)
1838   Lord Lindsay, *Letters on Egypt, Edom and the Holy Land,* 2 volumes (London)
1841   E. Robinson and E. Smith, *Biblical Researches in Palestine, Mount Sinai and Arabia Petraea: A Journal of Travels in the year 1838*
1843   W.H. Bartlett, *Walks About the City and Environs of Jerusalem* (London)
        The Rev George Fisk, *A Pastor's Memorial of Egypt, the Red Sea, the Wilderness of Sinai and Paran, Mount Sinai, Jerusalem, and other principal localities of the Holy Land visited in 1842* (London)
1844   J.T. Bannister, *A Survey of the Holy Land: Its Geography, History and Destiny* (London)
        J.W. Johns, *The Anglican Cathedral Church of St. James, Mount Zion, Jerusalem* (London)
1845   Lieutenant-Colonel George Gawler, *Observations and Practical Suggestions in Furtherance of the Establishment of Jewish Colonies in Palestine: The Most Sober and Sensible Remedy for the Miseries of Asiatic Turkey* (London)
        John Lowthian, *A Narrative of a Recent Visit to Jerusalem and Several Parts of Palestine in 1843-44* (London)
        The Rev George Williams, *The Holy City: or Historical and Topographical Notices of Jerusalem* (London)
1846   The Rev John Blackburn, *A Hand-book Round Jerusalem* (London)
        Dr Merryon (narrator), *Travels of Lady Hester Stanhope,* 3 volumes (Travels of 1812) (London)
1847   Dr John Kitto, *Modern Jerusalem* (London)
1850   The Rev Moses Margoliouth, *A Pilgrimage in the Land of My Fathers,* 2 volumes (London)
1851   W.H. Bartlett, *A Pilgrimage Through the Holy Land* (London)
1852   J. Finn, *Opening Address, Jerusalem Literary Society* (Beirut)
1853   Abbé Mariti, *Histoire de L'Etat Present de Jérusalem* (Paris)
        Titus Tober, *Denkblätter aus Jerusalem* (St. Gallen and Konstanz)
1854   *Shrines of the Holy Land Contested By the Russian and the Turk* (London)
        C.W.M. Van de Velde, *Narrative of a Journey Through Syria and Palestine in 1851 and 1852,* 2 volumes (Edinburgh and London)
1855   W.H. Bartlett, *Jerusalem Revisited* (London)
        The Jerusalem Miscellany (London)
1856   Hanmer L. Dupuis, *The Holy Places: A Narrative of Two Year's Residence in Jerusalem and Palestine,* 2 volumes (London)
        The Jerusalem Miscellany, No. 2 (London)
        Edward Robinson, *Later Biblical Researches in Palestine and the Adjacent Regions: A Journal of Travels in the Year 1852* (London)
        Auguste Salzmann, *Jérusalem: Etude Photographique des Monuments de la Ville Sainte* (Paris)
1858   Horatius Bonar, *The Land of Promise: Notes of a Spring Journey from Beersheba to Sidon* (London)
        James Graham, *Jerusalem, Its Missions, School, Converts etc under Bishop Gobat* (London)
1862   Frederika Bremer, *Travels in the Holy Land,* translated by Mary Howitt, 2 volumes (London)
1864   Ermete Pierotti, *Customs and Traditions of Palestine, Illustrating the Manners of the Ancient Hebrews* (Cambridge)
        Ermete Pierotti, *Jerusalem Explored* (London)
1865   Robertson and Beato, *Jerusalem Album Photographique* (Constantinople)
1866   William Hepworth Dixon, *The Holy Land,* 2 volumes (London)
        Mrs. Finn, *Home in the Holy Land: A Tale Illustrating Customs and Incidents in Modern Jerusalem* (London)
1867   Religious Tract Society, *Pictorial Journey Through the Holy Land, or, Scenes in Palestine* (London)
1873   Committee of the Palestine Exploration Fund, *Our Work in Palestine* (London)
1874   The Rev Samuel Manning, *Those Holy Fields* (London)
1875   Isabel Burton, *The Inner Life of Syria, Palestine and the Holy Land,* 2 volumes (London)
1876   Charles Warren, *Underground Jerusalem* (London)
1878   James Finn, *Stirring Times, or Records from Jerusalem Consular Chronicles of 1853 to 1856,* 2 volumes (London)
        Colonel Wilsson, *Picturesque Palestine, Sinai and Egypt,* 4 volumes (London)
1882   Felix Bovet, *Egypt, Palestine, and Phoenicia: A Visit to Sacred Lands* (London)
1883   The Rev Andrew Thomson, *In the Holy Land* (journey of 1869) (London)
1884   Col. Sir Charles Warren and Capt. Claude Reignier Conder, *The Survey of Western Palestine: Jerusalem* (London)
1885   Rev J. King, *Recent Discoveries in the Temple Hill at Jerusalem* (London)
1886   Walter Besant, *Twenty-One Years' Work in the Holy Land* (London)
1887   Cunningham Geikie, *The Holy Land and the Bible,* 2 volumes (London)
        Mark Twain, *The New Pilgrim's Progress* (London)

1888   Sir Richard Temple, *Palestine Illustrated* (London)
1889   Major C.R. Conder, *Palestine* (London)
1891   The Rev Hugh Callan, *The Story of Jerusalem* (Edinburgh)
        The Rev James Kean, *Among the Holy Places* (London)
        Ellen E. Miller, *Alone Through Syria* (London)
1893   G. Robinson Lees, *Jerusalem Illustrated* (London)
        W.M. Thomson, *The Land and The Book* (letters written in 1857) (London)
        L. Valentine (editor), *Palestine Past and Prest, Pictorial and Descriptive* (London and New York)
1894   Bishop John H. Vincent, (Photograph Artist, Robert E.M. Bain), *Earthly Footsteps of the Man of Galilee: Our Lord and his Apostles Traced with Note Book and Camera,* 2 volumes (St Louis, Missouri and London)
        Notes by English Visitors to Abraham's Vineyeard, near Jerusalem (London)
1898   Edwin Sherman Wallace, *Jerusalem the Holy* (Edinburgh and London)
1899   F.H. Deverell, *My Tour in Palestine and Syria* (London)
1901   Dwight L. Elmendorf, *A Camera Crusade Through the Holy Land* (London)
        H. Rider Haggard, *A Winter Pilgrimage* (London)
1902   John Fulleylove and John Kelman, *The Holy Land* (London)
        Guía de la Peregrinación Bascongada á Tierra Santa y Rome (Bilbao)
        Major-General Sir C.W. Wilson, *The Water Supply of Jerusalem* (London)
1903   Elizabeth Butler, *Letters from the Holy Land* (written in the 1890s) (London)
1904   Miss A. Goodrich-Freer, *Inner Jerusalem* (London)
        The Rev Frank Johnson, *Under Cross & Crescent* (London)
1905   Underwood and Underwood, *Jerusalem THrough the Stereoscope* (New York)
1906   A.C. Inchbold, *Under the Syrian Sun,* 2 volumes (London)
1907   J. Davies-Smith *Palestine Portrayed: A Reminiscence of a Recent Tour* (London)
1910   Robert Hichens, *The Holy Land* (London)
1911   G.E. Franklin, *Palestine Depicted and Described* (London and New York)
1912   Sir Frederick Treves, *The Land that is Desolate* (London)
1913   Stephen Graham, *With the Russian Pilgrims to Jerusalem* (London)
1915   H. Sacher, *A Hebrew University for Jerusalem* (London)
1917   Albert M. Hyamson, *Palestine: The Rebirth of an Ancient People* (London)
1918   Dr. E.W.G. Masterman, *The Deliverance of Jerusalem* (London)
        Basil Mathews, *The Freedom of Jerusalem* (London)
        J.E. Wright, *Round About Jerusalem* (London)
        Lieutenant-Colonel Pirie-Gordon (Military editor), *A Brief Record of the Advance of the Egyptian Expeditionary Forces* (Cairo)
1919   Norman Bentwich, *Palestine of the Jews* (London)
1920   Georgraphical Section, Naval Intelligence Division, Naval Staff, Admiralty, *A Handbook of Syria* (London)
1921   G.K. Chesterton, *The New Jerusalem* (London)
        Millicent Garrett Fawcett *Six Weeks in Palestine* (London)
1923   Richard Cadbury, *9000 Miles in the Track of the Jew* (London and Edinburgh)
1924   C.R. Ashbee (editor), *Jerusalem 1920-1922* (London)
        Myriam Harry *A Springtide in Palestine* (London)
1925   Israel Cohen, *The Journal of a Jewish Traveller* (London)
        Robert H. Goodsall, *Palestine Memories 1917-1918-1925* (Canterbury)
        Inauguration of the Hebrew University Jerusalem, April 1st, 1925 (Jerusalem)
1926   The Rev. J.E. Hanauer, *Walks in and around Jerusalem* (London)
1930   Cyrus Adler, *Memorandum on the Western Wall* (Philadelphia)
        Report of the Commission on the Palestine Disturbances of August 1929, Command Paper 3530 of 1930 (London)
1932   Norman Bentwich, *A Wanderer in the Promised Land* (London)
        Junior Hadassah, *A Primer on Palestine* (New York)
1933   E. Mills, *Census of Palestine 1931,* 2 volumes (Alexandria, Egypt)
        Mary Berenson, *A Modern Pilgrimage* (London and New York)
1935   Vincent Sheean, *In Search of History* (London)
1937   *Palestine Royal Commission Report,* Command Paper 5479 of 1937 (London)
1946   *Report of the Anglo-American Committee of Enquiry regarding the problems of European Jewry and Palestine,* Command Paper 6808 of 1946 (London)
        A Survey of Palestine prepared in December 1945 and January 1946 for the Information of the Anglo-American Committee of Inquiry, 2 volumes (Palestine)
1948   Henry Kendall, *Jerusalem The City Plan: Preservation and Development During the British Mandate 1918-1948* (London)
        Progress Report of the United National Mediator on Palestine, Command Paper 7530 of 1948 (London)
1950   Harry Levin, *Jerusalem Embattled: A Diary of City under Siege March 25th, 1948 to July 18th 1948* (London)
        Moshe Sharett and Aubrey S. Eban, *The Peace of Jerusalem* (New York)
1951   Pauline Rose, *The Siege of Jerusalem* (London)
1965   Henry Kendall, *Jerusalem Jordan: regional planning proposals* (London)
1967   Dr. Beno Rothenberg (editor) *Jerusalem A Pictorial Report* (Tel Aviv)
1968   Eli Landau, *Jerusalem The Eternal: The Paratroopers' Battle for the City of David* (Tel Aviv)
        Richard Westmacott, *Jerusalem, A New Era for a Capital City* (London)

1973   Arthur Kutcher, *The New Jerusalem: Planning and Politics* (London)
        Gideon Weigert, *Housing the East Jerusalem* (Jerusalem)
        Gideon Weigert, *Israel's Presence in East Jerusalem* (Jerusalem)
1976   *Projects of the Jerusalem Foundation* (Jerusalem)

PART THREE; Historical works, biographies and memoirs

Adler, Marcus Nathan, *The Itinerary of Benjamin of Tudela,* London 1907
Aref-el-Aref, *Dome of the Rock,* Jerusalem 1964
Amiran, David H.F. Sachar, Arie and Kimhi, Israel (editors), *Urban Geography of Jerusalem,* Berlin and
    New York 1973
The Architecture of Islamic Jerusalem, Jerusalem 1976
Bar-On, Brigadier-General Mordechai (editor), *Six Days,* Tel Aviv 1968
Ben-Arieh, Y., *A City Reflected in its Times: Jerusalem in the Nineteenth Century,* Part One: The Old
    City, Jerusalem 1977.
Ben-Eliezer, Shimon, *Destruction and Renewal, The Synagogues of the Jewish Quarter,* Jerusalem 1975.
Bentwich, Norman (editor), *Hebrew University Garland,* London 1952
Bentwich, Margery and Norman, *Herbert Bentwich: The Pilgrim Father,* Jerusalem 1940
Besant, Walter and Palmer, E.H. *Jerusalem, the City of Herod and Saladin,* London 1871
Bovis, H. Eugene, *The Jerusalem Question, 1917-1968,* Stanford, California 1971
Bridgeman, Charles Thorley, *The Episcopal Church and the Middle East,* New York 1958
Carpi, Daniel and Yogev, Gedalia (editors), *Zionism: Studies in the History of the Zionist Movement
    and of the Jewish Community in Palestine,* Tel Aviv 1975
Cattan, Henry, *Palestine and International Law,* London and New York 1973
Churchill, Randolph S. and Winston S., *The Six Day Way,* London 1967
Cohen, E., *The City in Zionist Ideology,* Jerusalem 1970
Comay, Joan, *The Temple of Jerusalem,* London 1975
Coquerel, Athanase Josue, *Topographie de Jerusalem au Temps de Jesus Christ,* Strasbourg 1843
Cromer, Ruby, *The Hospital of St. John in Jerusalem,* London 1961
Devon, F., *Issues of the Exchequer,* London 1837
Duncan, Alistair, *The Noble Heritage: Jerusalem and Christianity,* London 1974
Duncan, Alistair, *The Noble Sanctuary: Portrait of a Holy Place in Arab Jerusalem,* London 1972
Elath, Eliahu, *Zionism at the UN: A Diary of the First Days,* Philadelphia 1976
Eytan, Walter, *The First Ten Years: A Diplomatic History of Israel,* London 1958
Falls, Captain Cyril (maps compiled by Major A.F. Becke), *Military Operations Egypt & Palestine,* in two
    parts, together with a separate Map Case volume, London 1930.
Furneaux, Rupert, *The Roman Siege of Jerusalem,* London 1973
Greenstone, Julius H., *The Messianic Idea in Jewish History,* Philadelphia 1906
The Hebrew University Jerusalem: Its History and Development, Jerusalem 1948
Hyamson, Albert M., *The British Consulate in Jerusalem in relation to the Jews of Palestine 1838-1914,*
    Part I, 1838-1861; Part II, 1862-1914, London 1939
The Israel Exploration Society, *Jerusalem Revealed: Archaeology in the Holy City 1968-1974,* Jerusalem
    1975.
Israeli, Yael, *Jerusalem in History and Vision,* Jerusalem 1968
Join-Lambert, Michel, *Jerusalem,* London 1958
Joseph, Dov, *The Faithful City: The Siege of Jerusalem, 1948,* New York and Tel Aviv 1960
Katz, Samuel, *Battleground - Fact and Fantasy in Palestine,* New York 1973
Kenyon, Kathleen M., *Jerusalem: Excavating 3000 Years of History,* London 1967
Kisch, Lt. Colonel, F.H. *Palestine Diary,* London 1938
Kollek, Teddy and Pearlman, Moshe, *Jerusalem Sacred City of Mankind: a history of forty centuries,*
    London 1968
Kollek, Teddy and Pearlman, Moshe, *Pilgrims to the Holy Land: The Story of Pilgrimage through the
    Ages,* London 1970
Lauterpacht, Elihu, *Jerusalem and the Holy Places,* London 1968
Lorch, Lt. Colonel Netanel, *The Edge of the Sword: Israel's War of Independence, 1947-1949,* New York
    and London 1961
Lowenthal, Marvin, (editor), *The Diaries of Theodor Herzl,* London 1958
Macalister, R.A.S., *A Century of Excavation in Palestine,* London 1925
Newton, Frances E., *Fifty Years in Palestine,* London 1948
Oesterreicher, Monsignor John M., and Sinai, Anne (editors), *Jerusalem,* New York 1974
Oesterreicher, Monsignor John M., *Jerusalem the Free,* London 1973
Palmer, E.H. *A History of the Jewish Nation,* London 1874
Parkes, James, *The Story of Jerusalem,* London 1949
Pollack, F.W., *The Turkish Post in the Holy Land,* Tel Aviv 1962
Prawer, Joshua, *The Latin Kingdom of Jerusalem: European Colonialism in the Middle Ages,* London
    1972
Raphael, Chaim, *The Walls of Jerusalem: An Excursion into Jewish History,* London 1968
Reiner, Elchanan, *The Yochanan Ben Zakkai Four Sephardi Synagogues,* Jerusalem (no date)
Royaumont, Sieur de, *The History of the Old and New Testaments extracted from the Holy Fathers and
    other Ecclesiastical Writers,* London 1705
Rozin, Mordechai and Landau, Julian L., *Mishkenot Sha'ananim,* Jerusalem 1974
Sacher, Harry, *Israel: The Establishment of a State,* London 1952

Bibliography of Works Consulted (cont.) Part Three

Samuel, Viscount Edwin, *A Lifetime in Jerusalem,* London 1970
Schleifer, Abdullah, *The Fall of Jerusalem,* New York 1972
Schneider, Peter and Wigoder, Geoffrey, (editors), *Jerusalem Perspectives,* Arundel, 1976
Scholem, Gershon, *Sabbatai Sevi: The Mystical Messiah 1626-1676,* London 1973
Silver, Abba Hillel, *A History of Messianic Speculation in Israel,* New York 1927
Smith, George Adam, *The Historical Geography of the Holy Land,* London 1931
Smith, George Adam, *Jerusalem,* 2 volumes, London 1907
Stanley, Arthur Penrhyn, *Sinai and Palestine in connection with their History,* London 1905
Sukenik, E.L., and Mayer, L.A., *The Third Wall of Jerusalem: An Account of Excavations,* Jerusalem 1930
Undique ad Terram Sanctam Cartographic Exhibition from the Eran Laor Collection, Jerusalem 1976
Vester, Bertha Spafford, *Our Jerusalem,* Beirut 1950
Weizmann, Chaim, *Trial and Error,* London 1949
Weblowsky, R.J. Zwi, *Jerusalem: Holy City of Three Religions,* Jerusalem 1976
Whiston, William, (translator), *The Works of Flavius Josephus,* London 1844
Williams, Louis (editor), *Military Aspects of the Israeli-Arab Conflict,* Tel Aviv 1975
Wilson, Evan, M., *Jerusalem, Key to Peace,* Washington D.C. 1970
Wright, Thomas (editor), *Early Travels in Palestine,* London 1848

List of Sources for the Illustrations

C.R. Ashbee (editor), *Jerusalem 1920-1922:* Plate 11
W.H. Bartlett, *Jerusalem Revisited:* Plates 26 and 31
W.H. Bartlett, *Walks About the City and Environs of Jerusalem:* Plates 10,16,28 and 29
Bodleian Library, Oxford: Plate 21
Central Zionist Archives: Plates 12,17,30,33,67,107 and 112
Joan Comay, *The Temple of Jerusalem:* Plate 15
Elia Photo-Service, Jerusalem: Plate 47
Martin Gilbert: Plates 114,115 and 116
Ya'acov Harlap: Plates 99 and 100
The Israel Exploration Society: Plates 103 and 104
Israel Information, London: Plates 98 and 117
Israel Museum, Jerusalem: Plates 1,18 and 27
Jerusalem Municipality Archive: Plates 6,19,38,41,42,45,46,48,50,54 and 68
Jerusalem Post Picture Collection: Plate 82
Jewish Agency Photographic Service: Plates 23,32,49,55,56,63,75,76,79,81 and 95
Keren Hayesod, United Israel Appeal, Information Department Photo Archives: Plates 64,66,70,71,73, 74,80,83,84,108 and 111
Keren Kayemet Archive: Plates 57,59,60,61,62 and 65
Michiel Miloco, *Viaggio da Venetia al Santo Sepolcro:* Plate 25
John Murray, Publishers: Plate 7
Palestine Exploration Fund: Plates 34 and 35
Zev Radovan: Plates 90 and 92
Elchanan Reiner, *The Yochanan Ben Zakkai Four Sephardi Synagogues:* Plate 44
Ross Photo, Jerusalem: Plates 101 and 102
Sieur de Royaumont, *The History of the Old and New Testament Extracted from the Holy Fathers and other Ecclesiastical Writers:* Plate 2
David Rubinger: Plates 58 and 89
Hanna Safieh: Plates 51,52,53,69,77,78 and 109
Gershom Scholem, *Sabbatai Sevi:* Plate 24
Isidore Singer (Managing Editor), *The Jewish Encyclopedia:* Plates 13 and 14
State of Israel, Government Press Office, Photographic Department: Plates 3,5,72,85,86,87,88,91,93, 94, 96, 97, 105, 106, 110 and 113
Bishop John H. Vincent, *Earthly Footsteps of the Man of Galilee:* Plates 22, 37 and 43
Charles Warren, *Underground Jerusalem:* Plate 36
William Whiston (translator), *The Works of Flavius Josephus:* Plate 4
Colonel Wilson, *Picturesque Palestine:* Plates 20,39 and 40
Professor Yigael Yadin: Plates 8 and 9